HILLWALKING IN
SNOWDONIA

Crib Goch (route 11.2)

HILLWALKING IN
SNOWDONIA
by
Steve Ashton

2 POLICE SQUARE, MILNTHORPE, CUMBRIA, LA7 7PY
www.cicerone.co.uk

© Steve Ashton
First Edition 1988
ISBN 1 85284 008 0

Second Edition 2002   **09172260**
ISBN 1 85284 349 7

A catalogue record for this book is available from the British Library

ABOUT THE AUTHOR

Steve Ashton began walking and climbing in Britain in his early teens. By the
age of 17 he had made the first ascent of a grade VI rock climb in the Italian
Dolomites. He moved from his native Lancashire to North Wales in the 1970s,
initially to work as a climbing instructor but then as a freelance writer and
photographer. He has since written ten books on hill walking and moun-
taineering, including the now classic *Scrambles in Snowdonia* (Cicerone Press).
For several years he was the equipment editor then humour columnist for *High
Mountain Sports* magazine, and a regular contributor of adventure travel features
to *Country Living*. He has won several awards for his writing, including the
Outdoor Writers' Guild *Award for Excellence* in 1992, 1994 and 1998.

    He currently teaches playwriting at the Arden School of Theatre in
Manchester and is an actor with Cat's Eye Theatre Company.

Advice to Readers

Readers are advised that while every effort is taken by the author to ensure the
accuracy of this guidebook, changes can occur which may affect the contents. It is
advisable to check locally on transport, accommodation, shops, etc, but even right
of way can be altered.

The publisher would welcome notes of any such changes.

CONTENTS

GLYDERS

PREFACE

Thirty-seven years have elapsed since E.G. Rowland wrote *Hill Walking in Snowdonia*. In that time the mountain tops have changed hardly at all, but the same cannot be said of many of the paths used to ascend them. The time has come for a complete reappraisal.

I found I could not update the original text without destroying Mr. Rowland's entertaining style, which would have been unforgivable. Instead, I have started afresh, selecting routes of greatest appeal to today's hill walker and adopting a simple and concise method of description. Hopefully the inclusion of sketch maps and a four-fold increase in photographs will help you to read between the lines. Nevertheless, I am aware that the new *Hill Walking* makes a better companion on the hill than by the fireside. I apologise for that, but not for the mountains themselves which, however they might be described, are the true source of inspiration.

INTRODUCTION

The routes have been selected from four areas: Carneddau, Glyders, Snowdon, and Outlying Areas (comprising Moelwyns, Eifionydd, Rhinogs, Cader Idris, Arans and Arenigs). Each has its own peculiar charm.

Most first-time visitors congregate around Snowdon. All major paths are well worn and in constant use during weekend and holiday periods. Nevertheless, the scenery around this complex mountain is magnificent. Walks begin by winding pleasantly up valleys or rough grazing land but typically finish on rock ridges poised above cliffs.

The Glyders are the second most popular walking area. Set among impressive rock scenery, their routes are characteristically short but scrambly. Most of the interest centres on the ridges and rock-walled cwms of their northern side.

The Carneddau occupy a large part of northern Snowdonia. Though lacking the intricacy of the Glyders, they provide magnificent walking over domed summits and barren connecting ridges. As yet only the main ascent routes to Carnedd Llewelyn are heavily used, so there is plenty of opportunity for escape.

Mountains outside the three main areas are lower and generally less rugged. Fences, quarries and pine forests detract from otherwise shapely hills. But there are compensations; apart from a few popular routes most paths are little wider than sheep tracks, while it would be unusual to meet more than a handful of people all day.

APPROACHES AND ACCOMMODATION

CARNEDDAU

The Carneddau lie within a triangle of main roads connecting Bangor, Conwy and Betws y Coed. Public transport, rail or bus can be used to travel between Conwy and Bangor, or Conwy and Betws y Coed. But there is no regular bus service along the A5 between Capel Curig and Bethesda (infrequent service in summer).

Although routes begin from each side of the triangle, the most convenient base for a longer stay will be on the A5 between Capel Curig and Bethesda. Both villages offer basic amenities and accommodation, including campsites, bunkhouses, youth hostels (Capel Curig and Idwal), bed & breakfast, and hotels. Main campsites are marked on OS maps, otherwise enquire locally.

GLYDERS

This is a relatively small area, confined by roads connecting Bethesda, Capel

Curig and Llanberis. Most routes begin from Ogwen Cottage, on the A5 midway between Bethesda and Capel Curig. A regular bus service operates from Bangor as far as Bethesda, but only a limited summer service continues along the Ogwen Valley to Capel Curig. Similarly, the regular bus service from Caernarfon extends up the Llanberis Pass only as far as Nant Peris. In summer the Sherpa buses continue up the Llanberis Pass to Pen y Gwryd (connections to Capel Curig).

By far the best base will be in the Ogwen Valley. Basic amenities can be found in Capel Curig and Bethesda, at either end of the valley. Accommodation at or near these villages includes campsites, bunkhouses, youth hostels (Capel Curig and Idwal), bed & breakfast, and hotels. Similar accommodation will be found in and around Llanberis at Nant Peris. There is also a youth hostel at Pen y Pass and a hotel at Pen y Gwryd.

SNOWDON

Mountains of the Snowdon group lie within a triangle of roads linking Caernarfon, Pen y Gwryd and Beddgelert. Regular bus routes from Caernarfon extend only as far as Nant Peris and Beddgelert. However, in summer the Sherpa bus service completes the circuit around the mountain by linking Beddgelert and Nant Peris via Pen y Gwryd. This service is extremely useful, even to car owners, because it facilitates unusual combinations of ascent and descent routes.

The Llanberis Pass and Nant Gwynant (the valley between Beddgelert and Pen y Gwryd) are the best bases. Both have campsites and bunkhouse accommodation. There is

Descending Pen yr Ole Wen via route 3.1. Tryfan in the background

also an excellent forestry campsite about 1.5km from Beddgelert on the Caernarfon road. The usual bed & breakfast and hotel accommodation will be found in and around Llanberis, Beddgelert and Rhyd Ddu (limited). Cafes are to be found at Pen y Pass and – of all places – the summit of Snowdon. Convenient youth hostels are at Bryn Gwynant, Llanberis, Snowdon Ranger and Pen y Pass.

OUTLYING AREAS

Walks described in this section are usually approached on a daily basis from central areas. However, those wishing to base themselves locally for a few days will find Beddgelert the most convenient for Eifionydd and the Moelwyns (refer to notes on Snowdon area), and the larger town of Dolgellau for southern Snowdonia, which includes the Rhinogs, Cader Idris, Arans and Arenigs.

CHOOSING A ROUTE

Routes are introduced and described under regional headings (Carneddau South, Snowdon East, and so on). A sketch map showing the routes accompanies each regional introduction. Aided by this, you should be able to select an appropriate combination of ascent and descent (notes in the route summaries offer some suggestions).

Route summaries also indicate the likely duration of the walk. These estimates are very approximate, but should help you select a half- or full-day walk as required. Metric units have

been used throughout for compatibility with metricated OS maps. Should it be necessary, multiply by 3 and add a tenth for an approximate conversion from metres (m) to feet, and multiply by 5 and divide by 8 to convert from kilometres (km) to miles. A useful formula (Naismith's) for calculating the likely duration of a walk is to allow 1hr. for each 5km of the walk plus 1hr for each 600m of ascent. Make special allowances for sections of scrambling or other rough terrain, and add time for long rest stops.

FOLLOWING THE ROUTE

Ascent notes indicate the main turning points of the walk. Sections of a route that are obvious to follow are described only in the most general terms, whereas intricate sections – such as an approach over fenced land – will be described in detail. Words printed in **bold type** relate to key destinations and turning points. This should help you to confirm your position from time to time.

This guide is designed to be used in conjunction with the appropriate OS maps. Mountain groups 1 to 12 are conveniently mapped on Sheet 115 (Snowdon) of the 1:50,000 Landranger Series, but to follow routes within groups 13 to 15 you will also need Sheet 124 (Dolgellau) of the same series. For detailed route-finding the best maps are those of the 1:25,000 scale Outdoor Leisure Series for Snowdonia. Three of these maps are required for the entire area, although the most important mountain groups will be found on the Snowdon sheet.

Not all locations referred to in the descriptions are named on the 1:50,000 maps. However, it should not be too difficult to relate the sketch map to your OS map of either scale.

Grid references have been used to confirm the location of starting points. These numbers relate to a numbered grid which is overprinted on every map. The first three numbers fix the vertical line on which the point lies: the last three, the horizontal line. Intersection of the two lines locates the point to within about 100m. Only the first two numbers of each set are shown on the map – the third number is a decimal approximation between grid lines (i.e. for GR: 792 564 read '79.2 across, 56.4 up'). Recent OS maps describe how to locate a point on the map from its grid reference, otherwise use this example to check your calculations: the summit station on Snowdon is at GR: 609 543.

This guide is not a substitute for route-finding skills. Changes will take place on the mountain while the book is in your possession; paths will be re-routed, fences and stiles erected or removed, cairns built and dismantled. Besides which, on some of the less popular routes only competent use of a map and compass will guide you safely across featureless slopes when the mist descends.

PRECAUTIONS

A lengthy discussion on this subject is beyond the scope of a guidebook. However, the following notes may serve as a reminder.

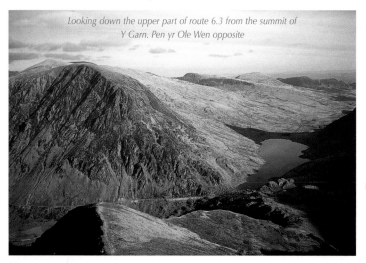

Looking down the upper part of route 6.3 from the summit of Y Garn. Pen yr Ole Wen opposite

WEATHER

Phone for a local weather forecast before setting out (consult the phone book or directory enquiries for the recorded forecast number). Remember that temperature decreases with altitude, and that wind speed and rainfall generally increase.

GROUND CONDITIONS

This book describes walks for *summer* conditions. The presence of ice and snow will transform a simple walk into a serious expedition requiring ice axe, crampons and a lot of experience.

EQUIPMENT

Everyone has personal preferences in this respect, but you might like to use this list as a reminder: boots, long socks, short socks, legwear, undershirt, midwear/pullover, windproof jacket, waterproof suit, hat, gloves, spare pullover, spare socks/gloves, map, compass, torch (with spare bulb and battery), whistle, food and drink, first-aid kit, survival bag, rucksack.

SCRAMBLING

During favourable weather, no route in this guide will tax the basic rock scrambling skills of an active hill walker. Nevertheless, accidents can and do happen because of loose rock, errors in route-finding, or simply through lapses in concentration. Summaries indicate if the walk includes a substantial section of scrambling. Avoid these routes in poor weather or if you feel uneasy about tackling rocks.

ACCESS

Access to the mountains of Snowdonia is not automatic. Some paths have been negotiated with landowners, others are used by unspoken agreement. In some areas, particularly Eifionydd and Aran, access remains an extremely sensitive issue. Inclusion of a route in this guide does not imply right of access. However, you are unlikely to be challenged on any of these walks provided you close gates after you, use stiles to cross walls and fences, and keep your dog on a lead.

ACCIDENTS

When practical it is a good idea to leave word of your intended route with someone at your place of accommodation. This will help the search party if you are long overdue and an accident is suspected. But don't forget to report back on your return! If you find yourself in difficulty on the mountain then try to attract attention by using the recognised distress signal: SIX SUCCESSIVE WHISTLE BLASTS OR TORCH FLASHES REPEATED AFTER A ONE-MINUTE PAUSE. If you need to call out the Mountain Rescue to help people injured or stranded on the mountain then dial 999 and ask for the police/mountain rescue.

CARNEDDAU

1: CARNEDDAU NORTH

1.1 walks the backbone of the range, nabbing a string of summits in the journey towards a distant Carnedd Llewelyn. 1.2 avoids main thoroughfares as much as possible, but cannot resist gawping at the impressive cascade of Aber Falls before wandering off to find solitude among the slopes of Drosgl. 1.3 combines the best of both routes and proves that all roads need not lead to Carnedd Llewelyn.

This is the empty quarter of the Carneddau. Tourists stroll up to Aber Falls come summertime, overlooked by lonely walkers strutting the ridge crest above, but otherwise the sheep have it to themselves. A green blanket lies over the land, hiding the interesting bits. Rugged scenery glimpsed by southern routes is absent; its grandeur is sensed emotionally rather than visually, as is often the case in regions of sweeping moorland. The sea adds another dimension to the view. It emphasises the shape and elevation of the land, sharpening the contrast between hills, broad and barren, and coastal plain, narrow and cluttered. Progress through this great expanse of rolling upland would be exasperatingly slow were it not for some excellent walking terrain. Short grass is kindest of all to tired feet.

1.1 CARNEDD LLEWELYN VIA DRUM

Summary:
A long, undulating ridge walk in remote surroundings. Much of the route is exposed to chilling and tiring cross-winds.

Duration:
12km and 1000m height gain – allow 5hrs plus descent time (3hrs by this route).

Terrain:
Stony track then excellent paths over grass or fine stones.

Approach:
From Bangor or Conway along the **A55** to **Aber**. From the village follow the narrow lane inland (marked 'unsuitable for coaches'), crossing the river at **Bont Newydd**, to a parking place (five cars) at its terminus (GR: 676 716).

Carnedd Llewellyn (left) and Yr Elen (right) from Foel Grach (route 1.1)

Ascent:

Go through the gate (Variant (a) goes left now) and ascend more or less directly to a wide track which contours the hillside below an initial spur of the ridge (ascended by Variant (b)). Turn right and follow the track to **Llyn Anafon**, a dammed lake nestling in the cwm below the steep west slope of **Drum**. Ascend this slope, reputedly by a path, directly to the summit.

Here is a good path, so follow it along the main ridge crest, crossing the summits of **Foel Fras** and **Foel Grach**. Route-finding is never difficult except under conditions of very poor visibility.

Finally ascend a scree dome to the summit plateau of **Carnedd Llewelyn**. Approach with caution: in mist you may not be able to find the actual summit or locate other ridges with certainty. Return by the same route if doubts remain.

Variant (a):

Turn left after passing through the gate and follow a track around the north side of the initial spur. Easy going but spoilt scenery. Turn right at **crossroads** and plod up a second track to its end not far short of the summit of **Drum**.

Variant (b):

Ascend the initial spur, trending left then right, to gain the ridge crest. Continue over several minor tops to the summit of **Drum**.

20

Descent:
This presents no special problems. Refer to ascent notes for directions.

Alternative Descents:
(1) 1.2 conveniently returns to **Bont Newydd** (park here if this is the plan). (2) Otherwise descend to Ogwen via the first part of 3.6, thus completing a full traverse of the Carneddau (return transport will be a problem).

1.2 CARNEDD LLEWELYN VIA ABER FALLS

Summary:
A wilderness walk beyond the popular spectacle of Aber Falls. Route-finding over the middle part will be frought with difficulties in mist; a good excuse to linger at the Falls before strolling back for an early lunch.

Duration:
11km and 1100m height gain – allow 5hrs plus descent (3hrs by this route).

Terrain:
Broad path to Aber Falls then intermittent paths over grass hillsides.

Approach:
From Bangor or Conwy along the **A55** to **Aber**. From the village follow the narrow lane inland (marked 'unsuitable for coaches') to a parking place (15 cars) by the bridge at **Bont Newydd** (GR: 662 720).

Ascent:
Go upstream along the riverside path, soon crossing at a wooden bridge to follow a broad track which leads up the far side of the valley to **Aber Falls**.

Ford the stream at boulders immediately below the falls – probably to the amusement of onlookers – to a grassy path opposite. Follow the path below **Rhaeadr Bach** (Little

Waterfall) to a second stream beyond a gate. Cross the fence at a poorly stile and ascend the stream bank to a shallow saddle, barren and boggy.

Turn left and ascend the open slopes of **Drosgl** (there is a grassy path if you can find it) to its summit perched on a huge mound of stones. Continue over the two minor tops of **Bera Bach** and **Yr Aryg**, each distinguished by rocky prominences, to a rock pile at the unpretentious summit of **Garnedd Uchaf**.

Aber Falls (route 1.2)

Walk south-east to locate the main ridge path and follow it, via **Foel Grach**, to the summit of **Carnedd
Llewelyn**.

Descent:
Avoid in mist. Otherwise it presents no particular
difficulty. Refer to ascent notes for directions.

Alternative Descents:
(1) 1.1 descends to the roadhead 1.5km beyond **Bont
Newydd**. (2) Refer also to 1.3. (3) A descent into Cwm
Eigiau via 5.1 will sustain the lonely atmosphere but incur
formidable transport problems.

1.3 DROSGL – FOEL FRAS – DRUM

Summary:
A satisfying circular walk among unfrequented hills.

Duration:
19km and 950m height gain – allow 7hrs (includes
descent time).

Terrain:
As for 1.1 and 1.2.

Approach:
As for 1.2.

Ascent & Descent:
As for 1.2 to **Garnedd Uchaf**. Walk east to find the main
ridge path, filter into the north-bound carriageway, and
descend by 1.1 over **Foel Fras** and **Drum** to the roadhead
at GR: 676 716. Walk/stagger down the cruelly inclined
tarmac road to **Bont Newydd**.

2: CARNEDDAU WEST

These routes journey through Cwm Llafar, or along one of its flanking spurs, and gain the high ridge crest which circles its head. This ridge is a major Carneddau highway. It links its two highest summits and intersects other important ridges, offering numerous opportunities for extending walks across the whole range.

Cwm Llafar penetrates deep into the heart of the Carneddau, almost severing the link between its two highest summits. A slender ridge remains, circling the cwm above a grim headwall known as the Black Ladders. A third summit, Yr Elen, dominates the north side of the cwm. Largely ignored, it is sometimes scooped up in a detour from Carnedd Llewelyn by peak baggers ticking down their list of the Welsh Threes (peaks above 3000ft). This is most unworthy of a fine mountain.

Intervening high ridges obscure views to the south, but views north may linger on the trackless Cwm Caseg and barren Drosgl dome beyond. Looking west the hills dip gently towards the coastal plain of the Menai Straits, their otherwise flawless green/brown skins blemished by a sprinkling of villages.

2.1 CARNEDD DAFYDD FROM GERLAN

Summary:
A pleasant and direct ridge walk up a thinly populated flank of the mountain. Unaccountably neglected.

Duration:
5km and 800m height gain – allow 3hrs plus descent time (1–2hrs by this route).

Terrain:
Mainly grass or stony paths. Some wet ground in the early stages.

Approach:
From **Bethesda** on the **A5**. Turn uphill from crossroads at the eastern town limit. Turn right at crossroads after 1km and find a parking place on the narrow lane, taking care not to obstruct gates or passing places.

Ascent:
The start is complicated. Continue along the road to the **water works** gate and go over a stile on the right. Cross a second stile at the top left corner of the field, and a third shortly after. Now follow the line of the stream, through a culvert, to open ground. Vague paths, parallel to the Afon Llafar, now rise steadily to a final stile (views into **Cwm Llafar**).

Continue along the path for a little

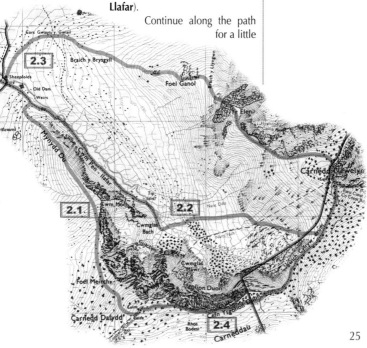

way then bear right (2.2 and 2.3 go their ways from here) to gain the right-bounding grass ridge of the cwm. Follow it throughout, over grass then boulders, to the scree summit dome of **Carnedd Dafydd**.

Descent:
When descending in mist, avoid straying onto false ridges leading down to cliffs which circle **Cwm Llafar**. Descent of the upper section is otherwise straightforward. In the lower part bear right off the ridge and follow the main **Cwm Llafar** path downhill. The route through lower pastures is easier to follow in descent (do not cross the Afon Llafar).

Alternative Descents:
(1) For the most convenient alternative descent, circle the head of **Cwm Llafar** to the shallow col of **Bwlch Cyfryw Drum** and return to Gerlan via 2.2. (2) Refer to 2.4 for a more satisfying circuit. (3) Combination with 3.6 and 4.2 gives a superb high-level traverse from Bethesda to Capel Curig (transport problems).

2.2 CARNEDD LLEWELYN FROM GERLAN

Summary:
A pleasant approach through a secluded valley with a final gruelling ascent towards the summit. Impressive cliff scenery at the head of the valley.

Duration:
7km and 825m height gain – allow 3–4hrs plus descent time (2hrs by this route).

Terrain:
Good path/track after an initial wet section, followed by a pathless and boulder-studded hillside. Scree path to finish.

Approach:
From **Bethesda** on the **A5**, as for 2.1.

Ascent:
The start is complicated – refer to 2.1 for details.

From the final stile enter **Cwm Llafar** along an excellent path/track and follow it to huge boulders below the sombre crag of **Llech Ddu**. Continue towards the head of the cwm, but trend left before it steepens to avoid the worst of a boulder field. Ascend eastwards up a steep and boulder-studded grass slope, well to the left of the **Black Ladders** cliff barrier, aiming to arrive on the ridge at the shallow col of **Bwlch Cyfryw Drum**. Turn left and follow the blunt ridge up to the **Carnedd Llewelyn** summit plateau.

Descent:
Refer to ascent notes (remember to bear right into **Cwm Llafar** before reaching the **Black Ladders** cliff barrier). The lower section is less obvious; refer to ascent notes of 2.1 for directions.

Alternative Descent:
2.3 conveniently returns to the start point, taking in **Yr Elen** on the way. However, in mist you may not be able to find the actual summit of Carnedd Llewelyn, which may make it extremely difficult to locate this descent. If in doubt return by the same route.

2.3 CARNEDD LLEWELYN
VIA YR ELEN

Summary:
Escapes a bog and follows a narrowing ridge over the fine satellite peak of Yr Elen. Captivating views down into lonely Cwm Caseg.

Duration:
6km and 900m height gain – allow 3–4hrs plus descent time (2hrs by this route).

Terrain:
Bog then a dry grass ridge. Stony paths in the upper reaches.

Approach:
From **Bethesda** on the **A5**, as for 2.1.

Ascent:
The start is complicated – refer to 2.1 for details.

Leave the path beyond the final stile (where 2.1 bears off to the right), roll up your trouser legs, and choose a suitable crossing of the Afon Llafar. Splosh north-east to emerge on the shallow left-bounding ridge of the cwm.

Follow the ridge crest, passing two rock prominences, until it curves to the right. Ascend very steeply near the blunt crest – slightly on the west side when in doubt – to the summit of **Yr Elen**. Circle south then south-east, around the head of **Cwm Caseg**, descending to a pronounced col. Follow the continuation ridge to a convex and featureless stone-studded slope leading onto the summit plateau.

Descent:
In mist the descent from the summit of **Carnedd Llewelyn** towards **Yr Elen** requires extremely careful navigation. Otherwise the route is obvious as far as the **Cwm Llafar** track (refer to ascent notes). Refer to the ascent notes of 2.1 for details of the lower section.

Alternative Descent:
2.2 conveniently returns to the starting point. If necessary the summit of **Carnedd Llewelyn** may be avoided by contouring south then south-east from the col above **Cwm Caseg** (faint path), arriving on the south ridge of **Carnedd Llewelyn** at **Bwlch Cyfryw Drum**.

2.4 CWM LLAFAR HORSESHOE

Summary:
An unfrequented ridge walk circling a remote cwm and visiting three major summits.

Duration:
14km and 1000m height gain – allow 5–6hrs (includes descent time).

Terrain:
As for 2.1 and 2.3.

Approach:
From **Bethesda** on the **A5**, as for 2.1.

Ascent & Descent:
As for 2.1 to the summit of **Carnedd Dafydd**. Circle the head of **Cwm Llafar**, east then north-east along a good ridge crest path, to the shallow col of **Bwlch Cyfryw Drum**. If bad weather develops the route can be abandoned here by descending 2.2, or shortened by taking the contouring traverse to the col above **Cwm Caseg** (though not in mist, when it would be difficult to locate). Continue up the broader ridge, as for 2.2, to the summit of **Carnedd Llewelyn**. In mist the descent from the summit of **Carnedd Llewelyn** towards **Yr Elen** requires extremely careful navigation. All being well, continue circling the cwm, via **Yr Elen**, as for 2.3 in reverse.

3: CARNEDDAU SOUTH

This is the familiar face of the Carneddau, rising gently northwards from the Ogwen Valley as a boulder-littered slope, bleached in the flat lighting. Hardly inspiring. But unseen from this viewpoint, tucked beyond the skyline ridge, are wild cwms and impressive crags which remain hidden until its crest is underfoot.

Most routes ascend a subsidiary ridge to reach the watershed between Ogwen and Conwy valleys. There is one exception. Some years ago a surfaced road was constructed directly up the hillside to Ffynnon Llugwy reservoir. It will never blend into the landscape and remains today as a monument to corporate insensitivity. We walk it with morbid curiosity.

The initial grind to gain height on these southern routes, debilitating in the full glare of a summer sun, is rewarded by unrestricted access to a network of high ridges. Here will be found excellent walking terrain, ideally suited for fast movers who like to traverse several summits in a day. As yet the majority of walkers seem unaware of these qualities, or else have been bewitched by Snowdon or the Glyders. Make the most of it before the word gets around!

3.1 CARNEDD DAFYDD FROM OGWEN COTTAGE

Summary:
A punishing ascent up the blunt south spur of Pen yr Ole Wen (best avoided on hot afternoons!) followed by a gentle ridge traverse. Compulsive retrospective views of the Glyders.

Duration:
3km and 800m height gain – allow 2–3hrs plus descent time (1–2hrs by this route).

Terrain:
Steep scree path with occasional boulder sections leading to a level stony path.

Approach:
From Capel Curig or Bethesda along the **A5**. Turn off at **Ogwen Cottage** to a car park with toilets, phone and

snack bar (GR: 649 604). Overspill parking in lay-bys to the east (note that parking tickets are served on motorists tempted by the run-in lane or broad pavements).

Descending Pen yr Ole Wen on route 3.1: a cloud sea fills the Ogwen Valley below

Ascent:
The start can be confusing. From the minor road exit go left along the A5 for a short distance, until over the bridge, and cross the Alfred Embleton **stile** on the north bank of the river. A rock slab, and possibly a bewildered school party, now bars the way. Climb the slab on polished footholds or, if shy, avoid it to the left or right (none too obviously). Trend left up the hillside to a level shoulder.

Follow the eroded path more or less directly up the broad spur, avoiding rock outcrops to right or left but never straying far from the crest (impressive views down left into gullies). Eventually the angle eases as the summit of **Pen yr Ole Wen** approaches.

Circle the rim of **Cwm Loer**, passing a huge cairn, to the summit stone pile of **Carnedd Dafydd**.

Descent:
Easy to follow (refer to ascent notes) but worryingly steep and loose.

Alternative Descents:
(1) A convenient and more pleasant alternative is to return to **Pen yr Ole Wen** and descend to Ogwen by 3.2 (one tricky scrambling section). (2) Otherwise descend 3.3 and walk back to **Ogwen Cottage** along the **A5** (4km). (3) Also refer to 3.6 for an extended ridge traverse which begins by ascending this route.

3.2 PEN YR OLE WEN FROM TAL Y LLYN

Summary:
A delightful and unjustifiably neglected route up the bounding ridge of a secluded cwm. Includes a short easy scramble.

Duration:
2.5km and 675m height gain – allow 2hrs plus descent time (1hr by this route).

Terrain:
Mostly good paths over grass and heather, plus a short rock scramble. Muddy at the start.

Approach:
From Capel Curig or Bethesda along the **A5**. Park on the roadside near the bridge at **Glan Dena** (GR: 668 605).

Ascent:

Follow the track across the bridge, passing the Hotel de **Glan Dena** (a modest wooden hut in days gone by), towards **Tal y Llyn** farm. Turn right just before entering the farm and cross the wall by a ladder stile. Continue directly up the hillside and cross the stream to follow its west bank. Leave it where the angle eases near the entrance to **Cwm Lloer** and head for the rock spur which defines the left side of the cwm. Climb it by a short gully and continue up a winding path near the crest to the summit.

Variant (a):

Follow the stream into **Cwm Lloer** and pass the lake on its south side. Avoid the rocks of Craig Lloer at the head of the cwm by zig-zagging steeply up an intermittent path on the scree and grass hillside to its right. The route emerges at a shallow col on the ridge between **Pen yr Ole Wen** and **Carnedd Dafydd**. Turn left to reach the summit.

Descent:
Most of the route is easy to follow in descent (refer to ascent notes). However, the scrambling section can be difficult to locate from above (take care not to veer onto crags on the north side of the spur). The upper section of the variant can look intimidating in descent – it is best avoided if unsure.

Alternative Descents:
(1) Usually down the south spur via the first part of 3.1 – unpleasantly loose and steep. (2) If this does not appeal then return by the same route, or through **Cwm Lloer** by the variant. (3) Alternatively, continue by 3.6 for a full circuit of the southern ridges.

3.3 CARNEDD DAFYDD VIA FFYNNON LLUGWY

Summary:
Initially a tedious road walk into an elevated cwm. Thereafter follows a little used spur to gain the main connecting ridge between Carnedd Dafydd and Carnedd Llewelyn, with fine views into Cwm Llafar.

Duration:
6km and 750m height gain – allow 3hrs plus descent time (2hrs by this route).

Terrain:
Surfaced road, grass, stony path.

Approach:
From Capel Curig or Bethesda along **A5**. Limited parking at the entrance to the private **Ffynnon Llugwy** access road (GR: 688 603), or at Gwern Gof Isaf farm (GR: 685 603).

Ascent:
Follow the access road to its terminus at the lake exit. Cross the outflow and ascend the spur, flanking terminal crags on their south side. Continue by an intermittent path up the broad crest of the spur to a junction with the main ridge path between **Carnedd Llewelyn** and **Carnedd Dafydd**. Turn left and follow it to the summit.

Descent:
The point of departure onto the spur from the ridge will be difficult to locate if it is misty. Lower down the spur, remember to veer south as the ground steepens to avoid terminal (!) crags above the lake. It must be said that a descent by this route lacks variety and invites blisters.

Alternative Descents:
(1) Descend to **Ogwen Cottage** by 3.1 or, better: (2) follow 3.1 to **Pen yr Ole Wen** and descend to **Glan Dena** via 3.2

3.4 CARNEDD LLEWELYN VIA FFYNNON LLUGWY

Summary:
A popular though inelegant beginning to a day on the Carneddau ridges. Unexpected views at Bwlch Eryl Farchog help to compensate.

Duration:
5km and 775m height gain – allow 3hrs plus descent time (2hrs by this route).

Terrain:
Surfaced road, stony paths, short rock scramble.

Approach:
From Capel Curig or Bethesda along the **A5**, as for 3.3.

Ascent:
Follow the access road for about 2km – a dehumanising grind – to where it veers left towards the lake exit. Leave it for a path which contours the hillside a few hundred

35

metres above the east shore of the lake. This path finally zig-zags steeply up to the col of **Bwlch Eryl Farchog**.

Turn left and follow the ridge, initially via a short rock scramble and later around the rim of Craig yr Ysfa's Amphitheatre, to the summit of **Carnedd Llewelyn**.

Variant (a):
Ascend 3.5 until near the summit of **Pen yr Helgi Du**, and then follow a narrow contouring path across its west face, arriving at the eastern extremity of **Bwlch Eryl Farchog**. Turn left and follow the ridge, rejoining the normal route shortly before its scramble.

Descent:
Take care to locate the correct line down to **Bwlch Eryl Farchog**. This simple scramble needs a steadying hand for just four or five metres – suspect a route-finding error if prolonged difficulties are met. A cairn on the col identifies the point of departure of the zig-zag path down to **Ffynnon Llugwy**.

Alternative Descents:
(1) To complete a mini-horseshoe descend the link ridge south then south-west towards **Carnedd Dafydd**, to where the spur of 3.3 breaks off to the left. Descend this back to the start. (2) Refer to 3.6 for a superior circuit.

3.5 PEN YR HELGI DU VIA Y BRAICH

Summary:
A straightforward ascent up a grass ridge to one of the Carneddau's outlying summits. More fun in descent.

Duration:
4km and 550m height gain – allow 2hrs plus descent time (1hr by this route).

Terrain:
Surfaced road, towpath (in a manner of speaking), yielding grass.

Approach:
From Capel Curig or Bethesda along the **A5**, as for 3.3.

Ascent:
Follow the access road to the **leat** bridge. Turn right and follow its south bank for about 0.5km. Cross by the second of twin footbridges to boggy ground on the right of a stone wall. Trend rightwards up the slope, later contouring right, to follow a path through a break in a transverse wall. Continue directly up the broad ridge to the summit plateau with cairns to left (the highest point) and right.

Descent:
Romp back down the ridge in a carefree manner until you arrive at a gap in the transverse wall. Now refer to the ascent notes to help you resist an apparent shortcut between leat footbridge and parking place (you'd get wet).

Alternative Descents:
(1) Scramble north-west down the ridge to **Bwlch Eryl Farchog** and descend via 3.4 (or continue by this route to **Carnedd Llewelyn** summit). (2) Alternatively reverse 4.2, over Pen Llithrig y Wrach, and return to the access road by following the leat 'towpath' throughout.

3.6 DAFYDD – LLEWELYN – HELGI DU

Summary:
A classic circular traverse; the best combination of southern ridges.

Duration:
16km and 1050m height gain – allow 6hrs (includes descent time).

Terrain:
Mostly excellent ridge paths over stony ground or grass plus a few sections of easy rock scrambling.

Approach:
From Capel Curig or Bethesda along the **A5**, as for 3.2.

Ascent & Descent:
Ascend **Pen yr Ole Wen**, as for 3.2. Continue via 3.1 to the summit of **Carnedd Dafydd**. Circle the Cwm Llafar rim to **Carnedd Llewelyn** summit. In mist the descent of 3.4 from **Carnedd Llewelyn** could be difficult to locate. Continue along the ridge to the far side of **Bwlch Eryl Farchog** and scramble pleasantly up to the summit of **Pen yr Helgi Du**. Descend 3.5 to the **A5**. Turn right and regain the start with 2km of unkind road walking.

Variant (a):
Avoid the scramble to **Pen yr Helgi Du** by contouring rightwards on to **Y Braich** from the eastern extremity of **Bwlch Eryl Farchog**. Shorter but inferior.

4: CARNEDDAU EAST

Among these mountains Pen yr Helgi Du is the best known. Sometimes it will be tacked onto a traverse of Carnedd Dafydd and Carnedd Llewelyn, the scramble to its summit and subsequent descent of Y Braich proving to be unexpected highlights of the day.

Pen Llithrig y Wrach hardly seem worth bothering with – despite an enigmatic name (the Witch's Slide?). Seen from the A5 it appears as little more than a bump on the skyline. But from this lowly viewpoint a rising moor conceals the bleak lake of Llyn Cowlyd, slopping below the mountain's precipitous south-east face and lending a dramatic quality to the ascent.

The Creigiau Gleision, which rise from the opposite shore of Cowlyd with equal abruptness, have a more rugged nature. However, pretty Llyn Crafnant softens the flank by which they are normally climbed and so they can never be thought unfriendly.

Mountains in this part of the Carneddau barely get a second glance from motorists speeding up the Ogwen Valley out of Capel Curig. As mere outliers they suffer badly in direct comparisons with major summits to the west. Consequently they are seldom climbed – a situation for which we may be thankful.

4.1 PEN LLITHRIG Y WRACH FROM CAPEL CURIG

Summary:
An uncomplicated ascent to an outlying and little visited summit. Impressive downwards views of Llyn Cowlyd.

Duration:
4km and 575m height gain – allow 2hrs plus descent time (1hr by this route).

Terrain:
Muddy moorland paths, tufted grass, heather.

Approach:
From **Capel Curig**. Start from the **A5**, 1km north of **Capel Curig** (GR: 719 589). Parking for two cars 100m further north (or park in **Capel Curig**).

Ascent:

Go through the gate at the footpath sign and follow a diagonal path up the hillside (waymarked to Llyn Cowlyd). Continue, passing above the house at **Tal y Waen**, to a ladder stile accessing the moor. Follow a broad path, rising steadily uphill, to a stream and **concrete bridge**. Turn left along the line of a fence to a **wooden bridge** over a leat/stream inflow to **Llyn Cowlyd**.

Cross the bridge and ascend a grass knoll on the far side. Now bear right to ascend, pathless and breathless, up a steepening blunt ridge to the summit.

Descent:
Presents no complications (refer to ascent notes).

Alternative Descents:
(1) A descent to Llyn Eigiau via 5.3 completes an interesting traverse (but involves transport difficulties). (2) Refer to 4.2 for a more convenient extension.

4.2 PEN LLITHRIG Y WRACH – PEN YR HELGI DU

Summary:
A satisfying circuit over two outlying peaks of the Carneddau. Fine views into Cwm Eigiau.

Duration:
14km and 800m height gain – allow 5hrs (includes descent time).

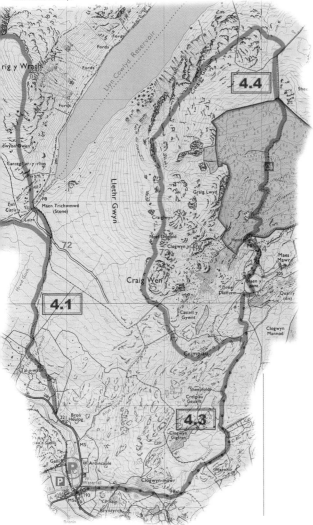

Terrain:
Muddy moorland paths, tufted grass, heather, excellent grass paths, leat 'towpath'.

Approach:
From **Capel Curig**. Start from the **A5**, 1km north of **Capel Curig** as for 4.1.

Ascent & Descent:
As for 4.1 to the summit of **Pen Llithrig y Wrach**.

Descend a shallow spur north-west from the summit to locate the narrow connecting ridge to **Pen yr Helgi Du**. Follow it, across **Bwlch y Tri Marchog**, to the broad and featureless summit plateau of **Pen yr Helgi Du**. The first cairn encountered is in fact slightly lower than the true summit, which lies at the north-west end of the plateau. When approaching in mist, consider ignoring the actual summit (it's nothing special) by circling the lip of **Cwm Bychan** to ensure locating **Y Braich** descent.

Descend due south as for 3.5, down the gradually dipping ridge of **Y Braich**, to a gap in the transverse wall. 3.5 now trends right; instead trend left, descending steep grass, to reach the **leat**. Cross it by the second of twin footbridges, turn left, and follow the 'towpath' to a junction with the ascent route at the **concrete bridge**. Resist shortcuts across bends in the leat; the intervening terrain gives extremely unpleasant walking over stubble and tufted marsh grass.

Return via the first part of 4.1 to the starting point.

4.3 CREIGIAU GLEISION FROM CAPEL CURIG

Summary:
Varied walking over a chain of miniature peaks. A route of surprising interest, with stunning views of familiar hills. Not recommended in misty weather because of intricate route-finding. An ascent to Crimpiau summit is rewarding in itself for a short day.

Duration:
6km and 650m height gain – allow 3hrs plus descent time (2hrs by this route).

Terrain:
Good paths over fields and moorland (some bogs), then rough ground with narrow paths.

Approach:
From **Capel Curig**. Start from Capel Curig Post Office on the **A5** (GR: 721 582).

Ascent:
Cross the stile opposite the Post Office and follow a path through fields and woodland passing to the north of the **Pinnacles** and to the south of **Clogwyn Mawr**. Cross the stream at a stone bridge and fork left. By-pass a boggy hollow on its east side and continue up to a shallow col and gap in a wall with views into the **Crafnant** valley.

Turn sharp left, through a gap in another wall, and continue ascending steeply. Circle the rim above **Crafnant** (no path) to a stony spine of a ridge. Follow this to the rock summit of **Crimpiau**.

The view west from Crimpiau (route 4.3). From left to right: Glyder Fach, Tryfan, Y Garn, Foel Goch (partially hidden), Pen yr Ole Wen

Descend steeply west then north-west to a marshy col. Ascend towards the next summit – **Craig Wen –** but detour west to avoid rocks. Regain the broad crest beyond and follow it slightly on the west side to the summit cairn of **Creigiau Gleision**.

Descent:
Refer to ascent notes.

Alternative Descent:
Return to **Capel Curig** via **Crafnant** (refer to 4.4).

4.4 CREIGIAU GLEISION AND CRAFNANT

Summary:
An extension to the Creigiau Gleision walk (4.3), returning via the picturesque Crafnant valley. A loud hailer could be useful for escaping the maze of forestry tracks, otherwise persevere with a 1:25,000 scale map.

Duration:
15km and 825m height gain – allow 5–6hrs (includes descent time).

Terrain:
As for 4.3 plus forestry tracks and poor paths over heather and tufted grass.

Approach:
From **Capel Curig** on the **A5**, as for 4.3.

Ascent & Descent:
As for 4.3 to the summit of **Creigiau Gleision**.

Descend north-east along the summit ridge (small path), passing over a subsidiary top, to a transverse post-and-wire fence. Turn right and follow it to where a collapsing fence arrives from the right. Turn right, follow a narrow path in heather alongside the fence, and go over a step stile at its end to enter a **forestry plantation**.

Crimpiau and Craig Wen (route 4.4) seen from Crafnant

Continue along a poor path through a break in the trees to a forestry track. Turn left and follow winding tracks until overlooking **Hendre**, or use shortcuts (unless paths have been obscured by recent felling) to descend directly. Pass **Hendre** on the left via a ladder stile, gate and foot-bridge. Fork right from the main track to **Blaen y Nant**, pass buildings on the right, and ascend to the viewpoint **col** of the ascent route. Return to **Capel Curig** as for 4.3.

45

5: CARNEDDAU NORTH-EAST

Each route in this section approaches its peak through Cwm Eigiau or along one of its flanking ridges. None sees much traffic, even in high summer. This is a good place to rediscover your hill walking roots.

Tantalising glimpses from neighbouring hills are often responsible for inspiring the first visit to a new area. But nothing overlooks this wild corner of the Carneddau except its own encircling rim of peaks. It does not advertise its qualities.

The approach along a narrow lane ends at the entrance to Cwm Eigiau, where marshland dips into the fringes of a shallow lake. A breached dam wall remains, apparently holding back nothing but a few acres of bog. Most of the wall is in good repair, although it no longer appears to serve a useful purpose.

A broad track extends along almost the entire length of Cwm Eigiau. It terminates at ruined quarry buildings in the wildest part of the valley. Pen Llithrig y Wrach and Pen yr Helgi Du rear up to the left, unexpectedly precipitous, while ahead rise the buttresses and gullies of Craig yr Ysfa, a major Carneddau climbing ground.

5.1 CARNEDD LLEWELYN VIA FOEL GRACH

Summary:
Ascends a little-used grass spur which penetrates into the heart of the Carneddau. Private yet spacious. Presents formidable route-finding difficulties in mist and is best avoided if bad weather is a possibility.

Duration:
8km and 825 height gain – allow 3–4hrs plus descent time
(2–3hrs by this route).

Terrain:
Mainly pathless moor grass. Stony path to finish.

Approach:
From Llanrwst or Conwy along the B5106 to Tal y
Bont. From the village follow a lane rising steeply
westwards for about 5km (**not** the road to
Llanbedr-y-cennin). Park at the roadhead at the
entrance to **Cwm Eigiau**, taking care not to
obstruct the gate (GR: 732 663).

Ascent:
Turn right, through the gate,
and follow a track across the
moor. Leave where it bends
sharp right and make

your way up on the ridge on the left (no path). Follow the ridge crest to a fine viewpoint at a small rock summit on its left side (a good place to squander a fine afternoon).

Cross the plateau south-west and ascend a blunt grass spur (signs of path) to **Foel Grach**. There is a refuge **hut** tucked under rocks on the north-east side of the summit.

Follow the main ridge path south to **Carnedd Llewelyn** summit.

Descent:
Uncomplicated in clear weather (refer to ascent notes).

Alternative Descents:
Transport difficulties severely restrict opportunities for descent into a different valley; a descent through **Cwm Eigiau** by Variant (a) of 5.2 conveniently returns to the starting point.

5.2 CARNEDD LLEWELYN
VIA CWM EIGIAU

Summary:
Delightful approach through a secluded valley escaped by heathery scrambling up the headwall. A typical Carneddau ridge completes the route. Variant (a) avoids the scramble but presents severe route-finding problems in mist.

Duration:
8km and 700m height gain – allow 3–4hrs plus descent time (2–3hrs by Variant (a)).

Terrain:
Rocky track (muddy in places), scree runnels through heather, simple rock scrambling, ridge path. Some boggy sections.

Approach:
From Llanrwst or Conwy along the B5106, as for 5.1.

Ascent:
From the roadhead continue directly ahead on a rough

track to the **Llyn Eigiau dam**. Cross the outflow on the left (5.3 bears off left soon after, along a higher track) and continue along a lakeside track. Later the track bridges the inflow and rises gradually across the far side of the cwm to a terminus at quarry building ruins with fine views ahead of **Craig yr Ysfa**. The scramble to **Bwlch Eryl Farchog**, though less difficult than appearances suggest, does require steadiness. If doubts remain follow Variant (a). Otherwise proceed as follows.

Fork right along a narrow path shortly before reaching the ruins (Variant (a) continues along this path), but leave it after a few metres to cross marshland on the left by a raised dyke. **Craig yr Ysfa** rises in front. A scree filled rift divides the cliff into two buttresses. Cross the stream and strike uphill to below the lowest rocks of the left-hand buttress. Skirt them on the left and discover a path going up left below the line of the crags. Follow it, zig-zagging up scree runnels in the heather, to a scrambling leftward exit. Follow the path left to a scree-filled trough and go up this, passing a solitary sapling. Trend left over heather and rock ribs to **Bwlch Eryl Farchog**.

Turn right and follow the ridge crest, over a short easy scramble and around the lip of Craig yr Ysfa's Amphitheatre, to the summit of **Carnedd Llewelyn**.

Variant (a):
Fork right just before reaching the quarry building **ruins** and follow a narrow path (which later disappears) up the right side of a stream towards the foot of a blunt grass spur. Continue as for 5.1, via **Foel Grach**, to the summit of **Carnedd Llewelyn**.

View down into Cwm Eigiau from Carnedd Llewelyn (route 5.2)

Descent:
Not recommended for descent except by Variant (a). This
is simple to follow in good visibility (refer to ascent notes)
but becomes a tricky navigational exercise in bad.

Alternative Descent: 5.1 returns to the starting point.

5.3 PEN LLITHRIG Y WRACH FROM LLYN EIGIAU

Summary:
An unfrequented ridge approach to an outlying peak of
the Carneddau. Fine views across Cwm Eigiau to Carnedd
Llewelyn.

Duration:
5km and 425m height gain – allow 2–3hrs plus descent
time (1–2hrs by this route).

Terrain:
Muddy track then clumpy grass with intermittent path.

Approach:
From Llanrwst or Conwy along the B5106, as for 5.1.

Ascent:
Initially follow 5.1 but fork left beyond the **Llyn Eigiau
dam** on a track leading to **Hafod y Rhiw**. Bear left up the
hillside to gain the ridge above its first steep rise. Follow
the broad back of the ridge (intermittent path) to a final
steep section leading directly to the summit of **Pen Llithrig
y Wrach**.

Descent:
The upper section is obvious in descent (refer to ascent
notes). In the lower part avoid terminal crags of the ridge
by descending the **Eigiau** flank (if in doubt aim for the
building of **Hafod y Rhiw**).

Alternative Descents:
(1) 4.1 continues the theme but invites problems with

return transport. (2) Another possibility is to descend 4.1 to **Llyn Cowlyd**, follow the lakeside path to its north end, and then return over the lower part of the ascent ridge to **Hafod y Rhiw**. (3) Refer to 5.4 for a complete circuit of **Cwm Eigiau** beginning with this route.

5.4 CWM EIGIAU HORSESHOE

Summary:
A prolonged high-level ridge walk of sustained interest around remote Cwm Eigiau. Only the middle section is well used. There are few good escape routes if the weather suddenly deteriorates.

Duration:
18km and 1000 height gain – allow 6–8hrs (includes descent time).

Terrain:
Mainly grass ridges with few paths. Good paths in the middle section, which includes two easy rock scrambles.

Approach:
From Llanrwst or Conwy along the B5106, as for 5.1.

Ascent & Descent:
Ascend to **Pen Llithrig y Wrach** summit via 5.3. Continue by 4.2 to the summit of **Pen yr Helgi Du** and then scramble down its north-west ridge to **Bwlch Eryl Farchog** (emergency descent to the Ogwen Valley from here via 3.4). Continue to the summit of **Carnedd Llewelyn** as for 3.4.

Descend 5.1 back to the starting point.

Craig yr Ysfa and Carnedd Llewelyn (rear) seen from Pen Llithrig y Wrach (route 5.4)

GLYDERS

6: GLYDERS WEST

The main Glyders ridge pivots around Cwm Idwal before dipping coastwards as a grassy ridge punctuated by summits of progressively lower altitude. So deep is the rift between Glyder Fach and Y Garn that these western peaks may be considered a separate chain by themselves.

Llyn Ogwen and Y Garn

Y Garn is the only well-trodden mountain among the group. It is the nearest to Ogwen and to the Llanberis Pass, which accounts for much of its popularity. Unlike the others it boasts a separate identity; there are few mountains so distinctive or attractive as Y Garn viewed in morning light from the shores of Llyn Ogwen. Ascents from Ogwen begin by entering Cwm Idwal. In summer this impressive rocky bowl teems with bodies driven here, protesting or otherwise, in forty-seater coaches. At other times it is enchanting.

Elidir Fawr – second highest peak of this group – stands aloof. It is connected to the main ridge by a slender neck of grass. Rarely climbed in its own right, it must be included (often reluctantly) by everyone hoping to complete a traverse of the fifteen North Wales summits which exceed an altitude of 3000ft. Nevertheless, its inclusion in a circular walk adds variety to an ascent of Y Garn from the Llanberis side.

6.1 Y GARN FROM NANT PERIS

Summary:
A short route which ascends the pastoral southern flank of
Y Garn with little respite. Breathtaking views into rugged
northern cwms.

Duration:
5km and 825m height gain – allow 3hrs plus descent time
(2hrs by this route).

Terrain:
Mainly good paths, grass then stones. Some wet ground.

Approach:
From Llanberis or Capel Curig along the **A4086** to a car
park on the east side of **Nant Peris** (GR: 608 582).

Ascent:
From the car park turn right and follow the main road for
1km. Turn left to follow a track and then an obvious path,
crossing a subsidiary stream, up the right bank of the Afon
Las. Eventually (and not before time) the angle eases
where the path, now less well defined, crosses wet ground
to **Llyn y Cŵn**. Avoid boggy shortcuts across the angle
near the lake.

Turn left to follow an initially dreary path up towards **Y
Garn** summit. In the upper part follow a good path around
the rim of **Cwm Clyd** for the best views.

Descent:
Obvious in clear weather (refer to ascent notes). When
descending from the summit in mist, take not to circle too
far around the rim of **Cwm Clyd** or you could find yourself
on the difficult knife-edge of Y Garn's east ridge.

Alternative Descents:
(1) 6.3 or (2) 6.4 provide interesting descents via **Cwm
Idwal** into the Ogwen Valley. (3) Refer to 6.2 for an
alternative return to the starting point.

6.2 Y GARN – FOEL GOCH – ELIDIR FAWR

Summary:
A worthwhile continuation to the previous route (6.1), prolonging its elevated viewpoint and bagging two more major peaks for little extra effort.

Duration:
13km and 1125m height gain – allow 5–6hrs

(includes descent time).

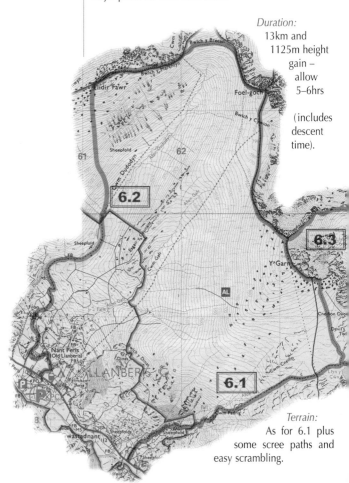

Terrain:
As for 6.1 plus some scree paths and easy scrambling.

Approach:
From Llanberis or Capel Curig along the **A4086** to **Nant Peris** car park, as for 6.1.

Ascent & Descent:
As for 6.1 to the summit of **Y Garn**.

   Descend the ridge northwards and fork left where it divides. Continue descending to a col. Ignore the main path which, since **Foel Goch** fails to reach the magic 3000ft, merely contours across its western flank, and instead ascend the ridge directly to its summit. Just one example of the many benefits of metrification.

   Descend the west ridge to regain the main path. Follow it, circling the head of **Cwm Dudodyn**, to the neck of the ridge leading up on to **Elidir Fawr**. Follow the ridge, mainly on its left side, to the elongated summit.

   Initially the descent from **Elidir Fawr** is very vague. The aim is to descend to the stream and path in **Cwm Dudodyn**, but a precise line on this featureless hillside is impossible to describe (take care in mist not to descend directly down the slope into an area of steep scree). However, consider following the summit ridge south-west until it starts to drop away, and then descend due south. If you can see it, a stile over a wall guides you on to a path. This in turn leads over a **footbridge** to the main path on the far side of the stream.

   Follow the path downstream. In a few hundred metres it trends left, away from the stream, and then zig-zags down the hillside. Shortly after crossing a stile, turn left to follow a track and surfaced lane into **Nant Peris**. Turn left at the main road and, provided you are not delayed at the Vaynol Arms, return to the car park.

6.3 Y GARN NORTH-EAST RIDGE

Summary:
The shortest and sweetest ascent of Y Garn. Wonderful views across Llyn Idwal towards the Idwal Slabs and Devil's Kitchen. The ridge is broader than appearances suggest and its ascent involves no genuine scrambling. Nevertheless, it is best avoided in high winds or if there is any risk of snowfall or frozen ground.

Duration:
3km and 650m height gain – allow 2 hrs plus descent time (1hr by this route).

Terrain:
Some boggy ground to start, then indefinite paths over grass and stones.

Approach:
From Capel Curig or Bethesda. Turn off the **A5** at **Ogwen Cottage** to a car park with toilets, phone and snack bar (GR: 649 604). Overspill parking in lay-bys to the east (note that parking tickets are served on motorists tempted by the run-in lane or broad pavements).

Ascent:
A path leads up a shale bank from the east (i.e. toilets) end of the car park. After a few metres it divides; take the right fork through a quarried canyon. Exit right from near its end and cross a ladder stile soon after. Continue on a less obvious path, over a second stile, until overlooking Llyn Idwal.

Trend rightwards over a grass dome, pass through a gap in a stone wall, and ascend towards a broad shoulder. This defines the right side of a stream which issues from **Cwm Clyd**. Zig-zag steeply up the shoulder to gain the barren ridge above. Follow the ridge, steepening, to its junction with the main ridge path between **Y Garn** and **Foel Goch**. Follow this up left to the summit.

Descent:
Not an ideal route of descent. The upper section is obvious to follow in clear weather (refer to ascent notes), although its appearance can be intimidating on first acquaintance. On the lower part of the ridge, trend right if in doubt to descend near the stream which issues from **Cwm Clyd**.

Alternative Descents:
(1) Descend 6.4 for a more satisfying circuit. (2) Alternatively descend into the Llanberis Pass via 6.1.

*Y Garn rising above
Llyn Idwal (route 6.3)*

6.4 Y GARN VIA DEVIL'S KITCHEN

Summary:
Wanders through Cwm Idwal, enjoying impressive rock scenery, then escapes from the Kitchen doorway up a cluttered ramp. Ends with a character-building pull to the summit.

Duration:
5km and 650m height gain – allow 3hrs plus descent time (2hrs by this route).

Terrain:
Unpleasant cobbled track then rocky paths. Paths over grass/bogs and stones to finish.

Approach:
From Capel Curig or Bethesda along the **A5**, as for 6.3.

Ascent:
A path leads up a shale bank from the east (i.e. toilets) end of the car park. After a few metres it divides; take the left fork, crossing a cute wooden bridge, to a rocky track. Follow the track, curving right, to **Llyn Idwal**.

Turn left and follow the lakeside path to the sweep of rock slabs. The path now rises diagonally rightwards, arriving at the entrance to the **Devil's Kitchen** with a scruffy scramble.

Ascend a crumbling ramp diagonally leftwards, and then follow a stone-filled runnel to **Llyn y Cŵn**. Turn right and follow the steepening path up to **Y Garn** summit. In the upper part follow a good path around the rim of **Cwm Clyd** for best views.

Variant (a):
From **Llyn Idwal**, cross the outflow by a footbridge and circle the lake by a constructed footpath on the far shore. Ascend a giant's staircase and continue through boulders to the **Kitchen** entrance (junction with the normal route).

Descent:
This route can be tricky in descent. Take care in mist not to circle too far around the rim of **Cwm Clyd** or you could find yourself on the difficult knife-edge of Y Garn's east ridge. From **Llyn y Cŵn** follow a path north-east to enter a stone-filled runnel. This leads down onto the ramp which slants down and across towards to the **Kitchen** entrance. The lower section is easy to follow (refer to ascent notes).

Alternative Descents:
(1) Combine with 6.3 for a more satisfying circuit of **Cwm Idwal**. (2) Alternatively descend into the Llanberis Pass by 6.1.

The ascent towards the Devil's Kitchen on route 6.4a

7: GLYDERS NORTH

Hanging valleys bite deep into the northern flank of the Glyders, exposing bony interiors from which streams gush to pool darkly in hollows beneath. It is a savage sight for eyes accustomed to rolling moorland landscapes.

Opportunities for conventional hill walks are limited by the ruggedness of the terrain. Three such routes find ways to skirt the main craggy frontage, ascending first to cols at either end of the main ridge, from where the summits may be approached more easily. Even so the Devil's Kitchen route succeeds only by following an improbable ramp line which cuts diagonally across the cliff barrier.

A broad, high-level ridge between Glyder Fach and Glyder Fawr links the two summits and sends down three slim, subsidiary ridges to the north. Each of these crests provides a scrambly walk. Permute any two of them for an interesting circuit from Ogwen Cottage.

7.1 GLYDER FAWR VIA DEVIL'S KITCHEN

Summary:
Degenerates into a sweaty struggle up scree paths after an interesting approach through Cwm Idwal. Wonderful rock scenery in Idwal and at the Devil's Kitchen.

Glyder Fawr seen from Cwm Idwal. Route 7.1 ascends the left-slanting ramp from below the dark cleft of the Devil's Kitchen (far right)

Duration:
4km and 700m height gain – allow 3hrs plus descent time
(2hrs by this route).

Terrain:
Unpleasant cobbled track then rocky paths. Punishing
scree paths to finish.

Approach:
From Capel Curig or Bethesda. Turn off the **A5** at **Ogwen
Cottage** to a car park with toilets, phone, and snack bar
(GR: 649 604). Overspill parking in lay-bys to the east
(note that parking tickets are served on motorists tempted
by the run-in lane or broad pavements).

Ascent:
A path leads up a shale bank from the east (i.e. toilets)
end of the car park. After a few metres it divides; take
the left fork and cross a
wooden bridge to a track.
Follow the track, curving
rightwards (7.3, 7.4, 7.5
and 7.6 break off left
here), to **Llyn Idwal**.
    Turn left and fol-
low the lakeside
path until below a
sweep of rock
slabs.

The path now rises diagonally rightwards, arriving at the entrance to the **Devil's Kitchen** with a scruffy scramble.

Ascend a crumbling ramp diagonally leftwards then exit up a stone-filled runnel towards **Llyn y Cŵn**.

Turn left about 100m before reaching the lake and follow a truly horrible scree path (some cairns) which winds up the broad south-west shoulder of **Glyder Fawr**. Turn left and follow the shoulder to a pile of rocks (one of several) at the summit.

Descent:
Can be difficult to locate in descent. From the summit descend the shoulder south-west for about 200m before turning north-west for the descent to **Llyn y Cŵn**. From **Llyn y Cŵn** follow a fpath north-east to enter a stone-filled runnel. This leads down onto the ramp, which slants down and across towards the **Kitchen** entrance. The lower section is simple to follow (refer to ascent notes).

Alternative Descents:
(1) Can be combined with 7.2 or 7.3, but in either case it would be better to use this route as the descent. (2) Refer to 7.6 for a complete circuit of **Glyder Fach** and **Glyder Fawr**.

7.2 GLYDER FAWR VIA CWM CNEIFION

Summary:
A little-used route, visiting a hanging valley high above Cwm Idwal and finishing with an easy scramble. Requires diligent route-finding to avoid difficult terrain lying to either side of the vague ascent line.

Duration:
3km and 700m height gain – allow 2–3hrs plus descent time.

Terrain:
Unpleasant cobbled track then vague paths over steep grass and rock hillsides.

GLYDERS NORTH

Approach:
From Capel Curig or Bethesda along the **A5**, as for 7.1.

Ascent:
As for 7.1 to the lakeside path in **Cwm Idwal**. Leave the path approximately midway along the lake. Ascend the steep hillside diagonally rightwards, passing to the right of a 100m rib of rock which protrudes from the slope. You should discover a small path contouring the hillside at about the level of the top of the rib; follow it rightwards towards **Cwm Cneifion**.

Enter the lower cwm and trend rightwards onto the broad shoulder which bounds its right side. Ascend its crest, dodging difficulties as necessary, to the summit dome and rock pile.

Descent:
A descent by this route is not recommended.

Alternative Descents:
(1) 7.3 preserves the scrambly nature of the ascent. (2) Alternatively, descend by 7.1.

7.3 GLYDER FAWR
VIA Y GRIBIN

Summary:
A fine ridge walk, culminating in a good scramble onto the main Glyders range.

Duration:
4km and 700m height gain – allow 3hrs plus descent time (2hrs by this route).

Terrain:
Stepping stones over boggy ground then eroded scree paths. A good ridge path with some rock scrambling to finish.

Approach:
From Capel Curig or Bethesda along the **A5**, as for 7.1.

65

Ascent:

As for 7.1 to where the track curves rightwards towards **Llyn Idwal**. Bear off left and follow the path, sometimes boggy (stepping stones), to a steep rise. Zig-zag up the eroded stream bank into **Cwm Bochlwyd**. Turn right and follow a path leading up onto the ridge which bounds the cwm on its right.

Follow a good path along the ridge to where it rears up into a final rocky prow. Scramble up its right flank, returning to the crest near the top.

Circle rightwards around the rim of **Cwm Cneifion** to join the main Glyders ridge path leading west to the summit rock pile.

Descent:

The top of the ridge can be difficult to locate when descending by this route in mist. The best strategy is to locate the rim of **Cwm Cneifion** and follow it (**not** too closely!) as it curves naturally onto the promontory above the ridge. Stay on the right side of the ridge in the lower section to be sure of locating the transverse path which leads across to the outflow from Llyn Bochlwyd. The lower section is obvious to follow (refer to ascent notes).

Alternative Descents:

(1) 7.1 is the usual descent. (2) Refer to 8.4 for a scrambling circuit of **Cwm Bochlwyd**, descending by this route.

7.4 GLYDER FACH VIA CWM BOCHLWYD

Summary:

A varied walk through impressive scenery. Cleverly avoids the difficult places.

Duration:

4km and 675m height gain – allow 3hrs plus descent time (2hrs by this route).

Terrain:
Stepping stones over boggy ground, eroded scree path, then good paths over grass and among boulders. A few metres of rock scrambling to reach the actual summit.

Approach:
From Capel Curig or Bethesda along the **A5**, as for 7.1.

Ascent:
As for 7.3 to **Cwm Bochlwyd**.

Cross the stream outflow and follow a path rising above the east shore of the lake to the pronounced col of **Bwlch Tryfan** (7.5 breaks off up to the right here).

Cross the wall by a ladder stile and follow a good path which contours around the head of **Cwm Tryfan**. Finally it rises to emerge on the grassy east shoulder of **Glyder Fach**. Turn right and follow a path up the shoulder, becoming rocky, to the summit plateau. Divert left for a photo opportunity at the Cantilever, or continue a little further to the summit rock pile.

Descent:
The actual summit rises from a rock-strewn plateau and can be difficult to locate in mist. Ignore it in bad conditions rather than risk losing the path. Take care not to stray onto paths which lead left onto **Bristly Ridge** or down the scree couloir on its east side. When certain of having passed that region, stay close to the north side of the ridge to be sure of locating the departure point of the traversing path which cuts back across to **Bwlch Tryfan**. From here the descent via **Cwm Bochlwyd** is more obvious (refer to ascent notes).

Alternative Descents:
(1) Any one of 8.5, 8.6, or 9.2 could be used for descent.
(2) Refer to 7.6 for a complete circuit of **Glyder Fach** and **Glyder Fawr** beginning with this route.

7.5 GLYDER FACH VIA BRISTLY RIDGE

Summary:
An exhilarating scramble up the pinnacled ridge above Bwlch Tryfan. Justifiably popular, though not a route to underestimate. The scrambling section is best avoided on windy days or if the rocks are wet (in which case follow Variant (a) or revert to 7.4).

Duration:
3km and 700m height gain – allow 3hrs plus descent time.

Descending into Great Pinacle Gap on Bristly Ridge (route 7.5)

Terrain:
As for 7.4 plus rock scrambling.

Approach:
From Capel Curig or Bethesda along the **A5**, as for 7.1.

Ascent:
As for 7.4 to **Bwlch Tryfan**.

Turn right at the stone wall and follow its right side up to the base of the first crags of the ridge. Go to the right about 10m and enter a short gully. Go up the gully and exit left at its top over a man-made wall. Above is a sinister-looking gully. Scramble up its bed until it steepens uncomfortably. Go left to a rib, up a little, and then back right to easier ground. Continue up a slabby shoulder to a narrowing of the ridge.

Scramble over a small pinnacle and then up to the top of a larger one. Descend into Great Pinnacle Gap. Scramble up a short wall on the far side, just right of the slender Great Pinnacle, to enter a recess. Pass through a gap between the squat pinnacle on the right and the main body of the ridge on the left. Easy ground leads up to a raised crest which delivers you onto the summit plateau.

Walk south-west to join the main ridge path. Follow it over boulders to the summit rock pile in a few hundred metres, or divert left to discover the Cantilever.

Variant (a):
Cross the ladder stile at **Bwlch Tryfan** and then zig-zag up scree paths in a broad couloir on the east side of **Bristly Ridge**.

Descent:
This route is not recommended for descent, although Variant (a) could be used if necessary.

Alternative Descents:
(1) 7.4 conveniently returns to **Ogwen Cottage**. (2) Otherwise refer to 7.6 for a continuation over **Glyder Fawr**. (3) 8.4 incorporates this route in a consistent scrambling circuit of **Cwm Bochlwyd**.

7.6 THE GLYDERS FROM OGWEN

Summary:
A classic combination of routes over the two Glyders, exploring their rocky northern cwms and discovering natural rock sculptures along their connecting ridge. Route-finding in mist between the two Glyders can be difficult without prior knowledge of the terrain.

Duration:
10km and 775m height gain – allow 5–6hrs (includes descent time).

Terrain:
As for 7.6 and 7.1.

Approach:
From Capel Curig or Bethesda along the **A5**, as for 7.1.

View west from near the summit of Glyder Fach on route 7.6. Y Garn (left) and Pen yr Ole Wen (right)

Ascent & Descent:
Follow 7.4 to the summit of **Glyder Fach**.

Continue south-west along the boulder-strewn summit plateau towards the bristling crag of **Castell y Gwynt** (Castle of the Winds). Either scramble through a gap just

left of its summit and descend to a col on the far side, or make a descending detour south for about 100m, returning to the col after passing beyond the crags.

Follow a path across the southern flank of the ridge, first through a muddy rut then over stones, to the summit of **Glyder Fawr**. Descend via 7.1, through **Cwm Idwal**, back to **Ogwen Cottage**.

8: GLYDERS EAST

Tryfan is something special. Isolated from the main Glyders ridge, this famous and popular peak has everything you could wish for in a mountain. Even by the easiest route you will find yourself scrambling over boulders and balancing across rock edges. The North Ridge, profiled to such good effect during the approach from Capel Curig, provides the most continuous scrambling ascent. In combination with an ascent of Glyder Fach by Bristly Ridge, and a descent of Y Gribin, it begins an outing comparable to the Snowdon Horseshoe. Cwms to either side of Tryfan add their own possibilities. Permutations of ascent and descent routes run into dozens.

A long, undulating ridge to the east will attract your attention when you have grown weary of the heavy traffic on Tryfan and Glyder Fach. Paths here are reminiscent of those in the quieter parts of the Carneddau or Moelwyns. They have barely worn through the grass mantle. Discover through them that solitude can sometimes be enriched by the proximity of crowds.

Glyder Fawr (left) and Y Garn (right) seen from the summit of Tryfan

8.1 TRYFAN NORTH RIDGE

Summary:
A famous ridge scramble to the finest summit in North Wales. Best avoided on windy days or when the rocks are wet.

Duration:
1.5km and 600m height gain – allow 2–3hrs plus descent time.

Terrain:
Paths over scree and heather then bare rock ridges.

Approach:
From **Capel Curig** or Bethesda along the **A5** to a lay-by with parking for several cars below the **Milestone Buttress**, a prominent rock face on the lower west side of the North Ridge (GR: 663 603).

Ascent:
Cross a stile at the lay-by and ascend a staircase on the left side of a stone wall. Trend left shortly before reaching the **Milestone Buttress** and ascend scree and boulders to the top of the first shoulder on the North Ridge (views down east to the slabs of **Little Tryfan**).

Detailed route-finding is intricate from here on, although the best line rarely deviates more than a few metres from the crest (several paths leave the ridge to follow inferior flanking lines across the upper part of the East Face).

Ascend more or less directly up the blunt ridge to a level section (the Cannon can be found over on the right). Proceed slightly left to a rock pavement and continue by easy scrambling beyond another level section.

The ridge suddenly narrows and rears up as a clean rock rib. Ascend it by the easiest line and descend into a notch beyond (or avoid this tricky section by a short detour to the left). Scramble out of the notch to gain the North Summit. Continue easily along the crest to the main Central Summit, identified by the twin standing stones of

Adam and Eve. The traditional leap from one to the other is optional!

Descent:
This route is not suitable for descent.

Alternative Descents:
(1) 8.2 or 8.3 both provide convenient returns to the start.
(2) Otherwise descend 8.3 to **Bwlch Tryfan**, 7.4 to **Cwm Bochlwyd**, and return to the start via the latter part of 8.4.
(3) Refer to 8.4 for an extended scramble over **Glyder Fach**.

8.2 TRYFAN VIA HEATHER TERRACE

Summary:
An improbable route based on a ramp which slants across

the precipitous East Face. Energetic in places, although sections of genuine scrambling are short.

Duration:
2.5km and 600m height gain – allow 2–3hrs plus descent time (1–2hrs by this route).

Terrain:
Rough paths over scree, rock and heather. Simple rock scrambling to finish. One boggy section.

Approach:
From **Capel Curig** or Bethesda. Roadside parking for many cars on the **A5** between **Gwern Gof Uchaf** and **Glan Dena** (GR: 671 605).

Ascent:
Walk east along the **A5** and turn right along a track to **Gwern Gof Uchaf**. Pass the farm on its left (stiles) and continue along a path to **Little Tryfan**, a unique sweep of rock slabs. Ascend below them then trend rightwards to follow a heathery path near a fence (Variant (a) arrives here from below). Ascend a prominent scree gully – some scrambling at the exit – to the indistinct beginnings of the Heather Terrace.

Follow the terrace leftwards, initially by some easy scrambling, until it becomes broader and more distinct. Continue until the terrace fades into a shallow depression beyond the cliff barrier. Ascend the depression to a prominent col on the South Ridge.

Cross the wall at a stile, turn right, and ascend the blunt South Ridge by its easiest line (some scrambling) to the South Summit. Continue to the main Central Summit with its standing stones of Adam and Eve.

8.6

Variant (a):
From the **A5**, cross a stile almost opposite the track to **Glan Dena** and follow an uphill path to join the normal route before it enters the scree gully.

Descent:
Refer to the ascent notes for directions on the upper and lower parts. The Terrace itself is surprisingly difficult to locate in descent. Look carefully for signs of path on the left (looking out) while descending the shallow depression from the South Ridge. If you miss the turning it might be better simply to continue downhill into **Cwm Tryfan** and return via 8.3.

8.3 CWM TRYFAN AND TRYFAN SOUTH RIDGE

Summary:
The least popular of Tryfan's normal ascent routes. A pleasant rocky finish compensates for limited views and muddy paths in the early stages.

Duration:
4km and 600m height gain – allow 2–3hrs plus descent time (1–2hrs by this route).

Terrain:
Muddy paths through heather. Easy rock scrambling to finish.

Approach:
From **Capel Curig** or Bethesda along the **A5**, as for 8.2.

Ascent:
Approach **Little Tryfan** as for 8.2, but veer left just before reaching it (i.e. shortly after walking along a rock pavement) to ascend steep grass on its left side. The path asserts itself soon after. Cross the fence at a stile beyond the summit of **Little Tryfan** and continue into **Cwm Tryfan**. Rampant heather makes for hard going in Cwm Tryfan if you stray from the path.

Follow a path up the right side of the cwm (some boggy sections). The path steepens at the head of the cwm to a junction with the contouring path of 7.4. Turn right and follow the path to **Bwlch Tryfan**.

Cross the wall at **Bwlch Tryfan** by a ladder stile and ascend stone paths and rocks of the South Ridge, usually on its west side, to the South Summit. Continue to the main Central Summit, where you will find the twin standing stones of Adam and Eve.

Descent:
A descent of the South Ridge is complicated by the sudden and frequent appearance of vertical drops. Have patience; most can be avoided on the west flank. Turn left at **Bwlch Tryfan**, crossing a ladder stile, and initially follow the contouring path above **Cwm Tryfan**. Leave it for a path which descends into the cwm. Trend right when paths divide in the lower part of the cwm and head for the knoll which marks the summit of **Little Tryfan**. Take the path on the boring side of **Little Tryfan** to return to **Gwern Gof Uchaf**.

Alternative Descents:
(1) 8.2 conveniently returns to the start. (2) Otherwise retrace the ascent route back to **Bwlch Tryfan**, descend 7.4 to **Cwm Bochlwyd**, return to the **A5** by the latter part of 8.4, and finally walk east along the road for about 1km to regain the starting point.

8.4 CWM BOCHLWYD HORSESHOE

Summary:
A splendid ridge capturing the essence of adventurous hill walking in the Glyders. Demands a genuine enthusiasm for scrambling. The difficult scrambling sections are all taken in ascent; nevertheless, the route is best tackled in fine weather when the rocks are dry.

Duration:
8km and 900m height gain – allow 6–7hrs (includes descent time).

Terrain:
Rough paths over rock and heather. Rock scrambling.
Some boggy ground near the finish.

Approach:
From **Capel Curig** or Bethesda along the **A5**, as for 8.1.

Ascent & Descent:
Ascend the North Ridge of **Tryfan** as for 8.1.

Descend the South Ridge to **Bwlch Tryfan** as for 8.3. If
conditions deteriorate the route can be abandoned here
by descending into **Cwm Bochlwyd**.

Ascend **Bristly Ridge** to **Glyder Fach** summit as for 7.5.
Continue south-west and scramble over **Castell y Gwynt**

*Castell y Gwynt on the
ridge between Glyder
Fach and Glyder Fawr.
Snowdon in the
background*

to the col beyond. Ignore the main path to Glyder Fawr and circle the rim of **Cwm Bochlwyd** onto the promontory above **Y Gribin**.

Descend **Y Gribin** to **Cwm Bochlwyd** as for 7.3. Descend an eroded path on the west bank of the stream issuing from **Cwm Bochlwyd**. Leave the path where it starts to level out and trend right, crossing the stream, to pass below **Bochlwyd Buttress**. Continue in the same line, descending diagonally across boggy ground, to a shallow ridge of grass and boulders. Descend this to the west of a large car park. Turn right on the **A5** and regain the starting point in less than 0.5km.

8.5 GLYDER FACH VIA BRAICH Y DDEUGWM

Summary:
Pleasant walking up a gentle ridge to join the ordinary route up Glyder Fach at half height. Superb views of Tryfan's East Face.

Duration:
4km and 700m height gain – allow 3hrs plus descent time (2hrs by this route).

Terrain:
Paths over grass then over scree and boulders. One very boggy section at half distance. Easy scrambling up the summit rock pile.

Approach:
From **Capel Curig** or Bethesda along the **A5** to park at the entrance to **Gwern Gof Isaf** farm (GR: 685 603), or in lay-bys further west.

Ascent:
Follow the track towards the farm and pass it on the right by crossing a stone wall at a ladder stile. Cross a second stile on the left and ascend the ridge by a path on the east side (or continue directly up the crest). The ridge leads out onto a grass plateau which harbours **Llyn Caseg-fraith**.

Ascend westwards (try not to be sucked into one of the many bottomless bogs hereabouts) to a path which ascends over boulders to the summit plateau. Veer left from the path to discover the Cantilever or continue to the summit rock pile.

Descent:

Route-finding in mist on the summit is extremely difficult. It may be better to ignore the summit rock pile than risk losing the path. Take care not to stray onto paths leading left onto **Bristly Ridge**, or down the scree couloir on its east side. The lower section is easy to follow (refer to ascent notes).

Alternative Descents:

(1) Descend 7.4 to the contouring path above **Cwm Tryfan**. Follow it for a few hundred metres then turn right and descend **Cwm Tryfan** as for 8.3. Just before reaching the farm at **Gwern Gof Uchaf**, turn right along a green track and follow it for about 1km back to the starting point. (2) Descend 8.6 to the track near **Gelli** but, instead of following it down into **Capel Curig**, turn left follow it for

Tryfan seen from Llyn Caseg-fraith at the convergence of routes 8.5 and 8.6

about 4km back to **Gwern Gof Isaf**. (3) Refer to 7.4 for other possibilities.

8.6 GLYDER FACH FROM CAPEL CURIG

Summary:
A long, undulating ridge walk followed by a bouldery ascent to the summit plateau. Not often used.

Duration:
8km and 925m height gain – allow 4hrs plus descent time (3hrs by this route).

Terrain:
Grass then paths over scree and boulders. One very boggy section. Easy scrambling up the summit rock pile.

Approach:
From **Capel Curig** on the **A5**. Car park.

Ascent:
Turn right from car park entrance and follow the lane uphill. Continue through a gate, passing the track junction leading left to **Gelli** farm, to where a higher track arrives from the left at a ruined stone building. Leave the track here and follow a vague path winding up to the left, through crags, onto the broad initial spur of the ridge. Continue along a narrow path, mostly on the left side of crest and over several minor summits, to the boggy col at **Llyn Caseg-fraith**. If conditions deteriorate, abandon the route here and descend 8.5 to **Gwern Gof Isaf**. Otherwise continue to the summit of **Glyder Fach** as for 8.5.

Descent:
The upper section is easy to follow in clear weather (refer to ascent notes), but refer to 8.5 for caution when descending in mist. In the lower section it can be difficult to find a way through the terminating crags of the ridge. If in doubt, quit the ridge sooner rather than later and

The eastern arm of the Glyders (route 8.6) seen from above Capel Curig

descend to the track which runs along its north side. Turn right and follow it to **Capel Curig**.

Alternative Descents:
(1) Descend 8.5 to **Gwern Gof Isaf**. Turn right along the track and return to **Capel Curig** in 4km. (2) Refer to 7.4 for other possibilities.

9: GLYDERS SOUTH

It is difficult to imagine a less inspiring mountainside than the southern slope of Glyder Fach, particularly when viewed from the side window of a car while speeding through the rain between Capel Curig and Pen y Gwryd. Boulders add texture to an otherwise monotonous hillside of fern and heather, but the slender ridges and rock walled cwms which shape the northern flanks of the Glyders are entirely absent. An insignificant rock pimple above the slope proves to be the summit of Glyder Fach.

At Pen y Pass the equally unappetising south-east slope of Glyder Fawr comes into view. This scree-cluttered hillside rises from the deep V of the Llanberis Pass with such demoralizing steepness than even veterans of Pen yr Ole Wen's South Ridge will balk at the prospect.

9.1 GLYDER FAWR FROM PEN Y PASS

Summary:
Surprisingly pleasant walking up a shallow spur with views of Snowdon and the Llanberis Pass from unfamiliar angles. Difficult route-finding in mist.

Duration:
3km and 650m height gain – allow 2–3hrs plus descent time (1–2hrs by this route).

Terrain:
Narrow path over grass then boulders. There is a short boggy section near the start.

Approach:
From Llanberis or Capel Curig along the **A4086** to a car park (fee) at **Pen y Pass** (GR: 647 556). Arrive early to secure a place. Roadside parking here is illegal (tickets are served regularly), so when full park opposite the **Pen y**

Just three routes have been described in this section: one up each of the Glyders, and a circular walk combining the two. However, the walks make such clever use of the terrain that they are well worth doing. Once you get to grips with them you will discover all kinds of features – ridges, runnels, outcrops – where none was expected. Views from the Glyder Fawr route – of Snowdon, Crib Goch and the Llanberis Pass – are tremendous.

Gwryd (GR: 661 558) and walk up to **Pen y Pass** in 20 minutes.

Ascent:

Go through a gate at the west end of the youth hostel buildings and cross the wall by a ladder stile. The path now rises leftwards across the steep hillside, passes to the left of a knoll (divert right for a view of **Llyn Cwm y Ffynnon**), and then descends slightly to a boggy area.

Proceed north-west up a blunt spur (red marker spots on boulders), later trending rightwards up a steep rise to arrive on the south spur itself at a grass col.

Ascend a broad spur, passing to the right of the cliffs, with some rough walking over boulders near the top. Depending on the line chosen, the final 100m or so to the summit rock pile could be shared with the cairned path which ascends from Llyn y Cŵn.

Descent:
Not recommended in poor visibility. Take care to locate the correct spur for the initial part of the descent (i.e. not the Esgair Felen spur further west). Avoid crags in the middle section of the spur on the east side. Stay on the east side lower down to help locate the path descending towards **Llyn Cwm y Ffynnon**.

Alternative Descents:
(1) There are many possible descents to Ogwen (refer to 7.1), but these involve complicated transport arrangements. (2) One possibility is to descend to Llyn y Cŵn as for 7.1, and then return via 6.1 to Gwastadnant at the bottom of the Llanberis Pass. (3) Refer to 9.3 for a circular walk incorporating **Glyder Fach**.

9.2 GLYDER FACH FROM PEN Y GWRYD

Summary:
A pleasant if unexceptional ascent of Glyder Fach by its gentle southern slope. Fascinating rock scenery on the summit plateau, but it is a long time coming.

Duration:
4km and 700m height gain – allow 2–3hrs plus descent time (1–2hrs by this route).

Terrain:
Paths through grass, bogs, heather and boulders. Short rock scramble to the actual summit.

Approach:
From Llanberis or Capel Curig along the **A4086** to the **Pen y Gwryd** hotel at the junction between the **A4086** and **A498**. Free parking opposite the hotel or in lay-bys further east (GR: 661 558).

Ascent:
Walk along the **A4086** towards Capel Curig for about 100m and cross a stile on the left. Follow the path

northwards and cross the stream by a **footbridge**. Continue along the path, rising steadily over stones and grass, to the boggy plateau west of **Llyn Caseg-fraith**.

Turn left and follow a path over grass then boulders to the summit plateau. Divert left to discover the Cantilever, or continue to the summit rock pile.

Descent:
Route-finding in mist on the summit plateau is extremely difficult; it may be better to ignore the summit rock pile rather than risk losing the path. Take care not to stray onto paths leading left onto **Bristly Ridge** or down the scree couloir on its east side. Otherwise the route is fairly obvious (refer to ascent notes).

Alternative Descents:
(1) There are many possible descents to Ogwen (refer to 7.4), but these involve complicated transport arrangements. (2) Descend to Capel Curig via 8.6. (3) Refer to 9.3 for a circular walk incorporating **Glyder Fawr**.

9.3 GLYDERS FROM THE SOUTH

Summary:
A logical combination of routes on the south side of the Glyders. Prolongs time spent exploring rock formations on their communal ridge.

Duration:
10km and 800m height gain – allow 4–6hrs (includes descent time).

Terrain:
As for 9.1 and 9.2 plus some road walking.

Approach:
From Llanberis or Capel Curig along the **A4086** to the **Pen y Gwryd** hotel, as for 9.2.

Ascent & Descent:
Walk up the **A4086** to **Pen y Pass** (20mins). Ascend **Glyder Fawr** as for 9.1.

Follow the main ridge path eastwards, over stones then along a soily rut, to the col below **Castell y Gwynt** (Castle of the Winds). Scramble easily through a gap just right of its summit (or make a detour down to the right, ascending again when safely beyond the Castell) to gain the **Glyder Fach** summit plateau.

Descend to **Pen y Gwryd** as for 9.2.

Looking back towards Glyder Fach from Glyder Fawr on route 9.3

10: SNOWDON NORTH-WEST

Millions of visitors have begun their ascent of Snowdon from Llanberis, a town not yet at ease with its growing status as a tourist hot spot. Curiously the gigantic slate quarries which blight the hillside opposite have now become an attraction in themselves, both to rock climbers and to tourists. Near by, the Dinorwic hydro-electric power station squats in surreal harmony on the shore between blue-grey spoil heap and turbid lake.

The Snowdon Mountain Railway and the Llanberis Path (10.1) cross twice before reaching the summit, providing an opportunity for the two sets of pilgrims to exchange stares. Between them these two highways have so completely carved up this flank of Snowdon that 'real' hill walkers refuse to go anywhere near the place! This might explain why the true crest of the Llanberis ridge (10.2), a magnificent natural line of ascent, suffers almost total neglect.

Equally neglected are the shapely green tops which rise above the far side of the cwm. A circuitous route to Snowdon (10.4) begins here with the ascent of Moel Eilio, but even by themselves these hills make a pleasant afternoon's walk from Llanberis (10.3) – particularly when Snowdon itself is overburdened with people or clouds. The Snowdon Ranger path (10.5), one of the mountain's more popular routes, initially crosses the southern flank of this group from a starting point in the Cwellyn valley.

10.1 SNOWDON VIA THE LLANBERIS PATH

Summary:
The most popular route up Snowdon – although this has more to do with its gentle angle than any intrinsic interests. There are fine views of Clogwyn Du'r Arddu, a famous climbing ground. Proximity to the railway adds curiosity value. In common with other routes up Snowdon, special equipment and knowledge are required to negotiate this path safely in winter conditions.

Duration:
6km and 850m height gain – allow 3–4hrs plus descent time (2hrs by this route).

Terrain:
Gently angled and well-maintained stony track. No wet sections of note. Its unyielding surface can be tiring on the feet.

Approach:
From **Llanberis**. Turn off the **A4086** at the eastern limit of **Llanberis** town, down a minor road opposite the Royal Victoria hotel. The road soon narrows at a cattle grid and winds steeply uphill. Follow it for 1km to a parking space at GR: 582 589.

Ascent:
A signpost near the parking area points the way up a well-marked track. It rises steeply to begin with, but the angle soon eases. There are no route-finding difficulties. About 1km after passing beneath the **railway** track you will arrive at the refreshment shack of **Halfway House**, where you can revive flagging spirits with cups of their traditional lemonade.

About 1km beyond **Halfway House** the track bears left (ignore a right fork here) and rises steeply towards the ridge. Here it passes beneath the **railway** a second

The view east to Crib Goch (left) and Moel Siabod (right) from the summit of Snowdon (route 10.1)

time to sudden and dramatic views down into the Llanberis Pass. The ascent continues up the broad shoulder of **Crib y Ddysgl** to where several paths, but only one railway, converge. The

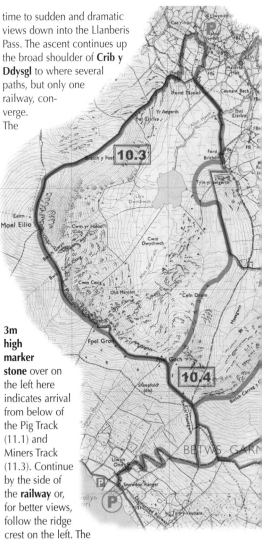

3m high marker stone over on the left here indicates arrival from below of the Pig Track (11.1) and Miners Track (11.3). Continue by the side of the **railway** or, for better views, follow the ridge crest on the left. The summit will be found under a large pile of bodies up to the left of the railway **station and café**.

Descent:

Initially descend on the right side of the **railway**. In mist take care not to stray onto the Snowdon Ranger path (10.5) where it diverges to cross the **railway** about 600m from the summit. The remainder of the route is simple to follow (refer to ascent notes).

Alternative Descent:
10.2 and 10.4 both provide alternative returns, but

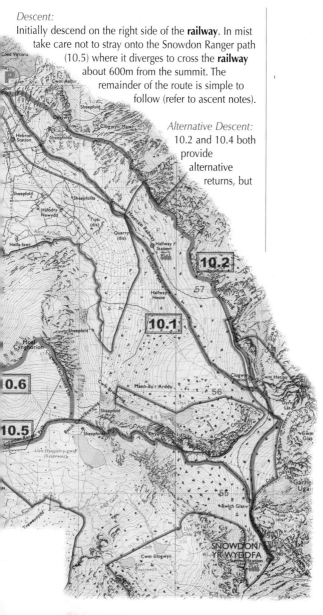

if considering such a combination it would be better to use this route as the descent.

10.2 SNOWDON VIA THE LLANBERIS RIDGE

Summary:
A peaceful alternative approach, on grass, to the upper part of the normal Llanberis Path (10.1). Breathtaking views down into the Llanberis Pass.

Duration:
6.5km and 875m height gain – allow 3–4hrs plus descent time (2hrs by this route).

Terrain:
Pathless grass ridge (some marshy cols) then stone tracks.

Approach:
From **Llanberis** on the **A4086**, as for 10.1.

Ascent:
A signpost near the parking area points the way up a well-marked track. Leave the track either just before or just after its initial steep rise, and then ascend grass on the left (no path) to gain the ridge crest.

Beyond its first minor top the ridge dips to a shallow, marshy col. Continue more steeply up the ridge, keeping to the left for best views. Beyond a second minor top the ridge rises steadily to a junction with the **railway** (divert left for impressive views from the rocky summit of Llechog).

Follow the **railway** to a junction with 10.1 at the bridge. Continue as for 10.1 to the summit.

Descent:
Initially descend on the right side of the **railway**. In mist take care not to stray onto the Snowdon Ranger path (10.5) where it diverges to cross the **railway** about 600m from the summit. Despite following a ridge, the lower

section can also be difficult to follow in mist because of the absence of cairns and paths (refer to ascent notes for general directions).

Alternative Descents:
(1) 10.1 offers the most convenient descent. (2) A descent by 10.4 – though much longer – is more in keeping with the theme of the ascent. In this case park in **Llanberis**, which is more convenient for the return, and walk up the minor road to the start of the path.

10.3 MOEL EILIO GROUP FROM LLANBERIS

Summary:
A delightful horseshoe walk over three summits. The tranquil setting more than compensates for lack of altitude.

Duration:
9km and 675m height gain – allow 4hrs (includes descent time).

Terrain:
Mainly grass. Stone track and surfaced lane to finish.

Approach:
From **Llanberis** on the **A4086**. Leave the by-pass and follow the old road into the village. Turn off the main street at GR: 578 601 along a narrow lane (Ffordd Capel Coch), passing the Chapel and ignoring a right turn. Continue along the surfaced road, ignoring a track which breaks off left to the **youth hostel**, to a limited parking space opposite a rubbish tip at GR: 573 594.

Ascent & Descent:
Walk back down the road for a few metres and turn left, crossing a ladder stile at a gate. Follow a rough track, curving left, and pass to the right of a cottage. Go through a gate and bear right to join the main contouring track at a gate and stile.

Cross the stile and turn left at once to ascend up grass (no path). Continue up the blunt ridge, staying on the right side of the wall/fence and crossing several stiles. Cross to the left side of the fence where the north ridge converges, arriving at the **Moel Eilio** summit circle shelter soon after.

Descend approximately south-east to a shallow col (intermittent path). Continue in the same line, ascending now, to the summit of **Foel Gron**.

Continue pleasantly around the rim of the cwm, soon descending to another grass col. Ascend the dome of **Foel Goch**, staying on the left side of a fence, to stiles at a junction of fences near the summit.

Ignore the stiles and turn left to descend the grass ridge northwards, following the left side of the fence. Cross the fence at a stile and follow the broad, level back of the ridge – over a second stile – until it begins to descend steeply. Avoid a terminating crag by a diversion to the left and descend to a track shortly before it passes the ruin at **Brithdir**.

Turn left to follow the track and surfaced lane, ignoring minor tracks at junctions, back to the start.

10.4 SNOWDON VIA MOEL EILIO

Summary:
A devious approach to Snowdon, crossing a range of miniature mountains on the way.

Duration:
12km and 1250m height gain – allow 6 hrs plus descent time (4hrs by this route).

Terrain:
Intermittent paths on grass then a broad stony path to finish.

Approach:
From **Llanberis** on the **A4086**. Park in **Llanberis** itself, which will be more convenient for a return by another

route, and walk up the narrow lane to the start of the path as for 10.3.

Ascent:
As for 10.3 to the summit of **Foel Goch**.

At the junction of fences, cross the stile in front (i.e. not the stile on the right) and turn right to follow the left side of the fence steeply down to **Bwlch Maes-gwm** – the Telegraph Col. Ascend the continuation of the ridge to the summit of **Moel Cynghorion**.

Descend steep grass of the south-east ridge to the pronounced col of **Bwlch Cwm Brwynog**. If the weather has deteriorated during a crossing of Moel Cynghorion then a sheltered descent to the north can be made from here down Cwm Brwynog.

Go a few metres right to join the Snowdon Ranger path (10.5). Follow this to **Snowdon** summit.

Descent:
There are no particular complications in descending this route in fine weather (refer to ascent notes), but refer to 10.5 for a note on descending the upper section in mist.

Alternative Descents:
(1) 10.1 provides the quickest return. (2) 10.2 is more in keeping with the atmosphere of the ascent route. (3) Combine with 11.5 or 12.2 for a magnificent traverse of **Snowdon**. During summer months it would be possible to return to **Llanberis** using the Sherpa bus service.

10.5 SNOWDON FROM THE SNOWDON RANGER

Summary:
A popular route up the comparatively gently west flank of the mountain. It contrives to avoid impressive views down the cliffs of Clogwyn Du'r Arddu – a short detour will remedy this oversight.

Duration:
6km and 950m height gain – allow 3–4hrs plus descent
time (2–3hrs by this route).

Terrain:
Mostly good paths. Some boggy sections in the lower
reaches.

Approach:
From Caernarfon or Beddgelert along the **A4085** to a large
car park opposite the **Snowdon Ranger Youth Hostel** (GR:
565 551).

Ascent:
Cross a stile opposite the car park to follow a marked path
and farm track. Zig-zag up the hillside behind the **farm**
until the angle eases (10.6 returns here after descending
from a col high up on the left). The path continues over
open moorland (some wet sections) and eventually rises
above the north shore of **Llyn Ffynnon y Gwas** to **Bwlch
Cwm Brwynog**, the col between **Moel Cynghorion** and
the main bulk of **Snowdon** (10.6 breaks off left here, 10.4
arrives).

Zig-zag steeply up the right flank of the ridge until the
angle eases (detour left for fine views down the cliffs of
Clogwyn Du'r Arddu). Continue along the stony path, rising steadily up the blunt upper part of the ridge, to a junction with a **railway** line. Follow the **railway** rightwards up
to the **station and café**. The actual summit lies a few
metres higher up on the left.

Descent:
Walk down the **railway**, ignoring the first marker stone
perched over on the right (this indicates departure of Pig
and Miners tracks), to a second marker stone shortly
afterwards. Bear left here, gradually veering away from the
railway. The remainder of the descent is simple to follow
(refer to ascent notes).

Alternative Descents:
(1) Initially by the same route but incorporating **Moel**

Cynghorion (refer to 10.6). (2) 12.4 descends to Rhyd
Ddu, 3km south of the youth hostel on the **A4085**, and is
therefore the most convenient alternative descent. (3) in
the summer months it would be possible, with a bit of
advance planning, to descend by almost any other route,
using the Sherpa bus service to return to the start.

10.6 MOEL CYNGHORION FROM THE SNOWDON RANGER

Summary:
A pleasant route over an unfrequented minor summit,
ideal for a short day or when thick cloud obscures the high
peaks.

Duration:
8km and 525m height gain – allow 3–4hrs (includes
descent time).

Terrain:
Good paths to start and finish (some boggy sections), but
pathless grass in the middle section.

Approach:
From Caernarfon or Beddgelert along the **A4085**, as for
10.5.

Ascent & Descent:
As for 10.5 to **Bwlch Cwm Brwynog**, the col between
Moel Cynghorion and the main bulk of **Snowdon**.
   Turn left and ascend a steep grass slope near its pre-
cipitous right edge (no path) to the broad summit area of
Moel Cynghorion.
   Descend a grass ridge approximately south-west then
west to **Bwlch Maes-gwm** – the Telegraph Col. Turn left
and follow the path down open grass slopes to rejoin the
Snowdon Ranger path just above its initial zig-zags. Turn
right and descend the zig-zags back to the car park.

11: SNOWDON EAST

Snowdon is at its best when viewed from the east, and from a distance. It can be seen standing proud above cliffs at the head of a sinuous cwm, its huge bulk balanced by the satellite peaks of Lliwedd and Crib y Ddysgl. Enter this eastern cwm and experience it for real – warts and all. Pipelines may clutter the floor of Cwm Dyli, synthetic paths may tame the headwall above Glaslyn, but the terrain mapped out by those enclosing ridges remains essentially rugged and no less fascinating.

The busiest route from this side of Snowdon is the Miners Track (11.3), winding its way up the valley floor to a terminus at disused copper mines below the headwall. The lakes of Teryn, Llydaw, and Glaslyn provide contrasting scenery to the jagged crests of encircling ridges. The Pig Track (11.1) contours the barren inner flank of Crib Goch (the north retaining ridge) and enjoys a bird's eye view of the Miners Track and its lakes.

Connoisseurs are drawn to this side of Snowdon by the ridge scrambles of Crib Goch and Lliwedd. The combination of the two – the famous Snowdon Horseshoe – is the finest outing of its type in Wales.

11.1 SNOWDON VIA THE PIG TRACK

Summary:
An extremely popular route despite an aimless beginning and a hideous finish up the engineered pavements of the Zig-Zags. Tremendous views across the cwm to Lliwedd and the north-east face of Snowdon.

Duration:
5km and 725m height gain – allow 3hrs plus descent time (2hrs by this route).

Terrain:
Well-maintained rocky path interspersed with a few rough sections on scree and rock.

Approach:
From Llanberis or Capel Curig along the **A4086** to a car park (fee) at **Pen y Pass** (GR: 647 556). Arrive early to secure a place. Roadside parking here is illegal (tickets are served regularly), so when full park opposite the **Pen y Gwryd** hotel (GR: 661 558) and walk up to **Pen y Pass** in 20 minutes.

Ascent:

From the upper car park follow the well-marked path westwards across the hillside above the Llanberis Pass. After about 1km it rises steeply to the pronounced col of **Bwlch y Moch** (views of **Lliwedd** rising beyond **Llyn Llydaw**). 11.2 bears off to the right here.

Continue along the main path, contouring the southern flanks of **Crib Goch**, to a promontory with fine views of **Glaslyn** and the north-east face of **Snowdon**.

The path now bears right to contour the head of the cwm (junction with 11.3) before rising steadily over rough ground to begin a clinical ascent of the **Zig-Zags**. The final section follows a narrow path, at first on bare rock, to emerge at a **3m marker stone**. Turn left and follow the ridge or **railway** track to the summit.

Left: Snowdon from the Pig Track (route 11.1)

Above: Glaslyn from the Pig Track (route 11.1). The shadowed ridge leading up to the right from beyond the lake is Y Gribin, taken by route 11.4. Lliwedd rises behind

Descent:
Look out for the **3m marker stone** at the exit of the **Zig-Zags** (you can hardly miss it!). Otherwise the route is simple to follow (refer to ascent notes).

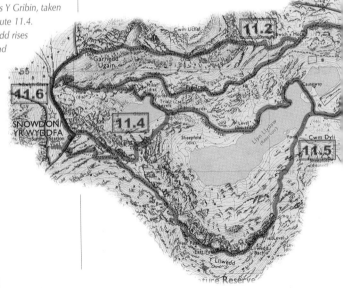

Alternative Descents:
(1) The most convenient descent is by 11.3 or 11.5 returning to **Pen y Pass**. (2) During summer months you could plan a descent by almost any other route, using the Sherpa bus service to return to **Pen y Pass**.

11.2 SNOWDON VIA CRIB GOCH

Summary:
A justly famous and popular ridge scramble. Not too difficult in good weather by the easiest route, but potentially dangerous in windy or freezing conditions.

Duration:
5km and 825m height gain – allow 4 hrs plus descent time.

Terrain:
Stony paths and bare rock ridges.

Approach:
From Llanberis or Capel Curig along the **A4086**, as for 11.1.

Ascent:
From the upper car park follow the well-marked path westwards across the hillside above the Llanberis Pass. After about 1km it rises steeply to the pronounced col of **Bwlch y Moch** (views of **Lliwedd** rising beyond **Llyn Llydaw**).

Turn right and follow a good path over the shoulder, heading for the blunt **East Ridge** of **Crib Goch**. Avoid an initial steep section on the left then ascend the ridge more or less directly. There is a junction with the **North Ridge** shortly before gaining the eastern extremity of **Crib Goch** itself.

View of the East Ridge of Crib Goch (route 11.2) from Bwlch y Moch

The main ridge traverse lies ahead. At first it is narrow and almost horizontal; follow it westwards, on or just below the actual crest, to the **Pinnacles**. Avoid a variant which descends several metres down to the left into a loose gully. Instead dodge through or over the **Pinnacles** with some exposed scrambling. An easy gully leads down to grass at **Bwlch Coch**. In an emergency the route may be quitted here – north-west towards **Llyn Glas**, or south towards **Glaslyn** (junction with 11.1 before reaching the lake). In either case take extra care in mist to avoid outcrops and steep scree.

Continue along the ridge, which soon becomes narrow and rocky again. Stay near the crest for the most interesting scrambling. The ridge broadens as it approaches the summit of **Crib y Ddysgl**.

Circle the lip of the **Glaslyn** cwm, descending steadily, to the **3m marker stone** at the exit of the Pig Track.

Beginning of the traverse of Crib Goch itself on route 11.2

Continue by the **railway**, or the ridge on its left, to
Snowdon summit.

Descent:
Not recommended as a normal means of descent.

Alternative Descents:
(1) The most convenient descent returns by 11.1 or 11.3 to
Pen y Pass (but see 11.6 for a more satisfying circuit). (2)
During summer months it would be possible to descend
by almost any other route, using the Sherpa bus service to
return to **Pen y Pass**.

11.3 SNOWDON VIA THE
MINERS TRACK

Summary:
A popular route following a broad track for much of its
length, initially among pleasant lake scenery. The final
steep section above Glaslyn is both tiring and unpleasant.
In doubtful weather, or if time is short, the walk up to
Glaslyn is rewarding in itself.

Duration:
6km and 725m height gain – allow 3hrs plus descent time
(2hrs by this route).

Terrain:
Well-maintained stony track. Some rough sections over
scree and rock.

Approach:
From Llanberis or Capel Curig along the **A4086**, as for
11.1.

Ascent:
The broad track starts from the far end of the lower car
park. Follow it throughout, contouring above **Llyn Teyrn**
and across the **Llyn Llydaw causeway**, to the north shore
of **Glaslyn**.

Ascend a steep scree and boulder slope to a junction with a traversing path – the Pig Track (11.1). Follow it to **Snowdon** summit.

Descent:

Look out for the **3m marker stone** at the exit of the **Zig-Zags**. Later the Miners Track breaks off and descends to **Glaslyn**. The division takes place where the Pig Track stops losing height after its descent of the **Zig-Zags** and begins to contour across a large scree tongue. This point is not obvious when descending in mist. The remainder of the route is simple to follow (refer to the ascent notes).

Sunlit buttresses of Lliwedd seen from Glaslyn on the Miners Track (route 11.3)

Alternative Descents:
(1) The most convenient alternative descent returns to **Pen y Pass** via 11.1. (2) During summer it would be possible to descend by almost any other route, using the Sherpa bus service to return to **Pen y Pass**.

11.4 SNOWDON VIA Y GRIBIN

Summary:
A scenic approach to a short but excellent ridge scramble. Similarly in difficulty to Crib Goch (11.2), but much less popular. Avoid in wet weather, when initial slabs in particular will feel insecure.

Duration:
6km and 725m height gain – allow 3hrs plus descent time.

Terrain:
Well-maintained track, rock ridge, scree and boulder finish.

Approach:
From Llanberis or Capel Curig along the **A4086**, as for 11.1.

Ascent:
As for the Miners Track (11.3) to **Glaslyn**.

Turn left and cross boulders at the **Glaslyn** outflow. Initially ascend over grass on the right side of the terminating shoulder of the ridge. Later trend left to reach the crest at a col below the steep part of the ridge.

Ignore loose flanking routes well right of the ridge and instead ascend scaly slabs slightly on the right of the crest. Continue approximately in the same line (some slight detours to the left) to a cairned promontory above the ridge. Trend slightly right to emerge at **Bwlch y Saethau**. Turn right and scramble easily (but with some loose rock) up the blunt ridge to **Snowdon** summit. Alternatively, descend slightly on the south side of **Bwlch y Saethau** to gain the Watkin Path (12.1) and follow this to the summit.

Crib Goch (left) and Llyn Llydaw (below) seen from the top of Y Gribin (route 11.4)

Descent:
Not recommended for descent.

Alternative Descents:
(1) The most satisfying return to **Pen y Pass** will be via **Crib Goch** (11.2). (2) Alternatively return over **Lliwedd** by 11.5, perhaps omitting the ascent to **Snowdon** to avoid crowds.

11.5 SNOWDON VIA LLIWEDD

Summary:
Traverses the rocky ridges of a satellite peak before grinding up to the Snowdon summit. Less demanding than Crib Goch (11.2), but generally quieter.

Duration:
7km and 900m height gain – allow 4hrs plus descent time (3hrs by this route).

Terrain:
Well-maintained stone track then paths over scree and boulders. Some simple rock scrambling.

Approach:
From Llanberis or Capel Curig along the **A4086**, as for 11.1.

Ascent:
As for 11.3 to **Llyn Llydaw**.

Turn left just before reaching the lake and follow a path near the shore, passing a lakeside building (valve house for the piped outflow to Cwm Dyli Power Station). The path soon veers away from the lake and rises steadily to reach the crest of the north-east ridge (some scrambling).

Follow the ridge crest or its left side, over **Lliwedd Bach** (slight descent), to the summit of **Lliwedd East Peak**. Continue along the crest to the slightly higher summit of **West Peak**.

Descend the crest of the rocky north-west ridge (some scrambling), or more easily by its left flank, to a large cairn at **Bwlch Ciliau**. If necessary the route may be abandoned here by descending the Watkin Path (12.1) into Nant Gwynant. There is no easy descent to the north-east, although competent scramblers could descend **Y Gribin** (11.4) to **Glaslyn**.

Continue as for 12.1 to **Snowdon** summit.

Descent:
Refer to 12.1 for directions to **Bwlch Ciliau**. The remainder of the route is simple to follow (refer to the ascent notes).

Alternative Descents:
(1) The most convenient descent is by 11.1 or 11.3. (2) **Crib Goch** gives a more satisfying return to **Pen y Pass**. This combination is the Snowdon Horseshoe (11.6) in reverse. (3) During summer it would be possible to descend by almost any other route, using the Sherpa bus service to return to **Pen y Pass**.

11.6 SNOWDON HORSESHOE

Summary:
A magnificent ridge traverse. Includes several sections of interesting scrambling, none of which are excessively difficult in good conditions.

Duration:
12km and 1000m height gain – allow 7hrs (includes descent time).

Terrain:
Good stone paths/tracks, scree paths, and bare rock ridges.

Approach:
From Llanberis or Capel Curig along the **A4086**, as for 11.1.

Ascent:
All components of the Horseshoe are described elsewhere but will be summarised here for convenience.

From **Pen y Pass** ascend the Pig Track (11.1) to **Bwlch y Moch**. Turn right and follow 11.2 over **Crib Goch** and **Crib y Ddysgl** to **Snowdon** summit. If the weather deteriorates while on **Snowdon**, or if time is short, it would be wiser to descend via 11.1 or 11.3 rather than to press on and be forced to abandon the route at **Bwlch y Saethau** with no easy descent available to **Pen y Pass**.

Descend the Watkin Path (12.1), initially via the South Ridge, to **Bwlch Ciliau**. Traverse the ridges of **Lliwedd** to **Llyn Llydaw** as for 11.5. Return to **Pen y Pass** via the Miners Track (11.3).

12: SNOWDON SOUTH

The large height difference between Snowdon summit and Nant Gwynant, starting point for both Watkin (12.1) and South Ridge (12.2) paths, has its compensations in the rich variety of scenery that unfolds – from trees and waterfalls to high cwms and rock ridges. An ascent from Rhyd Ddu (12.4) is quite different. From here the summit appears as an uninspiring bump on the skyline – a sight guaranteed to erode resolve as you plod slowly up its featureless western flank. Persevere, because later you will be surprised by the sudden change in character where the path circles above the cliffs of Cwm Clogwyn to share a final rocky spine with the South Ridge route.

12.1 SNOWDON VIA THE WATKIN PATH

Summary:
A delightful walk through varied scenery, marred only by a scruffy finish up a slope of shattered rock. Note that even a light frost or sprinkling of snow makes this final slope extremely insecure.

Duration:
6.5km and 1025m height gain – allow 4hrs plus descent time (2–3hrs by this route).

Nant Gwynant is a beautiful place. Disused mines and quarries betray an industrial past, though none have been worked to the overwhelming extent of those above Bethesda, Llanberis or Blaenau Ffestiniog. Limited forestry interest also ensures that these hillsides are largely spared the visual discords of hard-edged conifer blocks. Here and there, patches of original woodland soften the transition between lush valley and barren mountain.

The Watkin Path just below Bwlch Ciliau, Yr Aran in the background

Terrain:
Good tracks and paths with a final broken section over rock and scree.

Approach:
From Beddgelert or Pen y Gwryd along the **A498** to a car park at **Bethania** (GR: 628 507).

Ascent:
From the car park, cross the road bridge to gain the west bank of the river and turn right to follow a narrow lane. Fork left after about 400m on a stony track and follow it throughout, passing waterfalls in the confined upper reaches, to a level section at the entrance to **Cwm y Llan** (12.2 and 12.3 bear left here).

Continue along the track, across a

bridge and passing a **ruined building**, to where it curves left around the **Gladstone Rock**. From here the track rises slightly to spoil heaps. Follow it, curving rightwards, and continue pleasantly by a path up the east side of **Cwm Tregalan**. An upper, bouldery section leads to a large cairn at **Bwlch Ciliau** (11.5 arrives here after its descent of **Lliwedd**).

Turn left and follow the contouring path to **Bwlch y Saethau** (or for better views follow the undulating ridge on the right). Ignore scrambly paths ascending directly up the blunt ridge and instead follow a rising path left over scree and short rocky sections. Emerge, doubtless relieved, on the south-west ridge at a **2m marker stone**. Turn right and follow this upper continuation of the **South Ridge** (12.2), snubbing the railway **station and café**, to **Snowdon** summit.

Descent:
Resist following the direct line between **Snowdon** summit and **Bwlch y Saethau**. This is steep and insecure. The correct route descends the ridge south-west from the summit for about 200m to a **2m marker stone**, which indicates the point of departure for the Watkin Path. The remainder of the route is simple to follow (refer to the ascent notes).

Alternative Descents:
(1) **Snowdon South Ridge** (12.2) offers the most convenient alternative descent.
(2) In summer you might take advantage of the Sherpa bus service and descend to

Rhyd Ddu (12.4), Snowdon Ranger (10.5) or Pen y Pass (11.1, 11.3 or 11.5).

12.2 SNOWDON SOUTH RIDGE

Summary:
An excellent ridge walk. Exposed to strong winds where the ridge narrows and becomes rocky in the upper reaches.

Duration:
6.5km and 1025m height gain – allow 4hrs plus descent time (2–3hrs by this route).

Terrain:
Mainly good tracks and paths.

Approach:
From Beddgelert or Pen y Gwryd along the **A498** to a car park at **Bethania** (GR: 628 507).

Ascent:
As for 12.1 to the entrance of **Cwm y Llan**.

Immediately on reaching the top of the rise, and before crossing the stream, bear left and follow a steep diagonal path to the course of the old tramway. Turn right and follow it for a few hundred metres to where a path bears left over the grassy hillside. Take the path, rising steadily, to reach the **South Ridge** just above **Bwlch Cwm Llan**.

Ascend the ridge by a good path near its crest. In the upper reaches it narrows to a rocky crest and then dips to the exposed col of **Bwlch Main** (12.4 arrives here). Continue with interest, first on the right flank then on the left, passing the railway **station and café** shortly before reaching **Snowdon** summit.

Variant (a):
Follow 12.4 from **Rhyd Ddu** to where it turns left at the swing gate at GR: 582 525. Follow the green track to the quarry and continue along a narrow path over slate spoil to **Bwlch Cwm Llan**. Continue as for the normal route.

Descent:
There are no route-finding complications (refer to the ascent notes for directions).

Alternative Descents:
(1) The Watkin Path (12.1) offers the most convenient alternative descent. (2) In summer you could descend to **Rhyd Ddu** (12.4), Snowdon Ranger (10.5) or Pen y Pass (11.1, 11.3 or 11.5) and return to **Bethania** on the Sherpa bus.

12.3 YR ARAN FROM NANT GWYNANT

Summary:
A short but very pleasant walk over a small satellite peak of Snowdon.

Duration:
9km and 700m height gain – allow 4hrs (includes descent time).

Terrain:
Stony track to start and finish. Poor paths over grass and stones in the middle section.

On the ascent of Yr Aran (route 12.3)

115

Approach:
From Beddgelert or Pen y Gwryd along the **A498** to a car park at **Bethania** (GR: 628 507).

Ascent & Descent:
As for 12.1 to the entrance of **Cwm y Llan**.

Immediately on reaching the top of the rise and before crossing the stream, bear left and follow a steep diagonal path to the course of the old tramway – a level track. Cross the track and continue uphill, following a stream course, to a cairn and a better path.

Ascend the right side of a spoil heap to a disused mine. By-pass spoil from a second mine on the right and zig-zag up steep grass (no path) to the ridge crest.

Turn right and follow the ridge crest, on the right side of a stone wall, using a vague path. The wall veers right; cross it at a ladder stile and continue up the ridge using a stony path to the summit of **Yr Aran**.

Return to the ladder stile and turn left, descending a stony path on the left side of the wall. Go over the wall at a break, shortly before arriving at a grass col, and cross a ladder stile on the right. Turn left immediately and follow the right side of the wall, rising a little at first then descending to a cairn at **Bwlch Cwm Llan**.

Turn right and descend, initially over stony ground, to join a broad grassy path – the approach to the **South Ridge** (12.2). Descend the path diagonally across the hillside to join the tramway. Follow the tramway track to a junction with the ascent route and return via this to **Bethania**.

12.4 SNOWDON FROM RHYD DDU

Summary:
A popular route up the featureless western slopes of Snowdon. Interest develops in the upper reaches where it circles the rocky headwall of a remote cwm to finish up a rocky ridge. The narrow upper part, in the region of Bwlch Main, is exposed to strong winds.

Duration:
6km and 900m height gain – allow 3–4hrs plus descent time (2–3hrs by this route).

Terrain:
Track then stone paths. Some boggy sections.

Approach:
From Caernarfon or Beddgelert along the **A4085** to a large car park on the main road a few hundred metres south of **Rhyd Ddu** village (GR: 571 526).

Ascent:
Follow a track from the north end of the car park for about 100m. Turn right at a gate and follow a stony track which passes a small quarry and winds steadily uphill.

After about 1.5km, and shortly after crossing a ladder stile at a gate, turn left through a swing gate onto a narrower path. Follow it over rough ground and up a steeper section onto the broad shoulder overlooking **Cwm Clogwyn**.

Circle the rim of the cwm and zig-zag up fenced paths. Continue by the rocky left side of the ridge to the narrow col of **Bwlch Main** (junction with 12.2). Continue dramatically on the right flank of the ridge before returning to the more gentle left side. Continue up the ridge, passing the railway **station and café** shortly before reaching **Snowdon** summit.

Descent:
There are no route-finding complications (refer to the ascent notes for directions).

Alternative Descents:
(1) The **South Ridge** (12.2) by Variant (a) offers the most convenient alternative descent. (2) Otherwise a descent of the Snowdon Ranger (10.5) returns to the road just 2.5km north of the starting point. (3) In summer it would be possible to descend to **Bethania** (12.1) or Pen y Pass (11.1, 11.3 or 11.5) and return to **Rhyd Ddu** on the Sherpa bus.

OUTLYING AREAS

13: MOELWYNS

Isolated pockets of activity disguise a general neglect of the Moelwyns. Paths to many of the summits, where there are paths at all, are often no wider than sheep tracks. Paucity of impressive rock scenery could account for the lack of interest, although the surfeit of bog and slate spoil has also been cited – and not without some justification. But it is unfair to compare this area on a one-to-one basis with Snowdon or the Glyders. Judged on its own merits this is ideal territory for the escapist walker.

Moel Siabod dominates the northern region. A fine mountain by any standards, an ascent via the waters of Llyn y Foel and the rocks of Daear Ddu is outstanding. On a good day the views of Snowdon from its summit are without equal.

Interest in the southern group concentrates on Cnicht and the two Moelwyns, Fawr and Bach. Ascents from the east are blighted (or enriched, depending on your point of view) by the remains of massive industrial exploitation. Ascents from the west, as described here, are more conventional and will surprise some by their rugged interludes.

13.1 MOEL SIABOD FROM PONT CYFYNG

Summary:
A circular route visiting the most interesting parts of the mountain. Includes some simple scrambling. Difficult route-finding in mist.

Duration:
10km and 750m height gain – allow 4–5hrs (includes descent time).

Moelwyn Mawr seen from the summit of Cnicht

Terrain:
Narrow paths over grass (some boggy sections), easy scrambling, forest tracks and paths.

Approach:
From **Capel Curig** or Betws y Coed along the **A5** to a car park opposite the **Tyn y Coed hotel** at GR: 733 574.

Ascent & Descent:
Turn right at the car park exit and walk along the A5 to **Pont Cyfyng**. Fork right on a narrow road, crossing the bridge, and fork right again on reaching houses. Ascend this surfaced but private lane up to **Rhos Farm**.

Pass through the farmyard and continue along a track over the moor. Fork left at the far side of the moor, over a stile, and follow a path skirting the right side of a **lake**.

Continue on a less obvious path through quarry buildings. Pass to the left of a water-filled pit and continue, rising below the south-east flank of the mountain, to a shallow col with views of **Llyn y Foel** and the ascent ridge beyond. Pass the lake on its right side and gain the foot of the

121

The Daear Ddu ridge rises beyond Llyn y Foel to the summit of Moel Siabod (route 13.1)

Daear Ddu ridge. Scramble directly up its rocky crest (or, with less interest, on its left side), finally trending left to reach the trig point perched on the summit rock pile.

Descend the rocky summit ridge north-east to a shallow col. Turn left and descend over boulders to grass. Descend diagonally over grass slopes, heading for a spur extending in the direction of **Capel Curig** (if in doubt aim directly for the east end of the twin lakes of **Llynnau Mymbyr** – or set a compass bearing to the same point). Follow the spur (vague path) and descend to the left near its end to cross a stile. Turn right and follow a stony track among trees, over two ladder stiles, to a **forestry track**.

Turn right and follow the **forestry track**, ignoring a left turn shortly after merging with a lower track, to its end. Continue along a woodland path overlooking a river, rising briefly but then descending to cross the river at a footbridge opposite **Cobden's Hotel**. Turn right along the **A5** to regain the start in a few hundred metres.

Variant (a):
From the summit, descend the north-east ridge – rock then grass – to a junction with the approach route at the fork in the moor track.

13.2 CNICHT FROM NANMOR

Summary:
A circular walk over a popular Moelwyns summit. Includes some simple scrambling.

Duration:
9km and 500m height gain – allow 3–4hrs (includes descent time).

Terrain:
Mainly good paths. Simple rock scrambling in places. Some boggy sections.

Approach:
From Beddgelert or Pen y Gwryd along the **A498**. Turn off on a minor road a few hundred metres south of **Bethania**. Follow it for about 2.5km to a section with roadside parking near the track to **Gelli Iago** (GR: 632 484).

Ascent & Descent:
Take the track towards **Gelli Iago** and cross a stream on

At the summit of Cnicht (route 13.2)

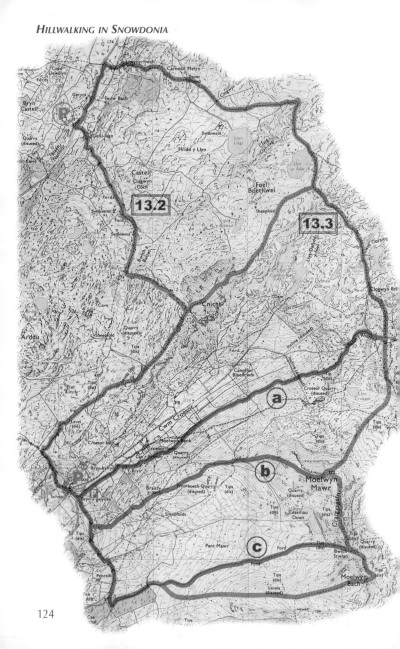

the right by a **footbridge**. Follow a winding path near the right bank of the stream to enter the upper cwm. Trend right near the head of the cwm to arrive at the shallow col of **Bwlch y Battel**.

Turn left and ascend a blunt ridge, steep and rocky, to a 'Lost World' **grass plateau** on the south-west ridge of **Cnicht** (junction with 13.3).

Turn left and scramble easily up the right side of the rocky ridge ahead to the summit of **Cnicht**.

Descend the north-east ridge, crossing or by-passing subsidiary summits, to a cairn at the far side of a **shallow col**. Turn left and descend to the east shore of **Llyn yr Adar**. Continue north-west, passing between outcrops, to a steep slope. Descend this, right then left, and follow paths on the right side of the stream outflow from **Llyn Llagi** (boggy moorland then pastures) to join the approach road. Turn left and walk back to the start in a little over 0.5km.

13.3 CNICHT AND THE MOELWYNS FROM CROESOR

Summary:
A circular walk over the three main peaks of the southern Moelwyns. Sudden contrasts in terrain and scenery maintain interest throughout. Difficult route-finding in mist.

Duration:
15km and 1000m height gain – allow 6hrs (includes descent time).

Terrain:
Stony track then paths over grass or rock. Simple scrambling in places. A few boggy sections.

Approach:
From Beddgelert or Penrhyndeudraeth along the **A4085**. Turn off about 0.5km north of **Garreg/Llanfrothen** village along the narrow **Croesor** road. Turn left at crossroads to a car park on the right, near the village (GR: 632 447).

Llyn Stwlan dam.
Moelwyn Bach (left)
and Craig Ysgafn
(right), traversed by
route 13.3, rise beyond

Ascent & Descent:
Turn right from the car park exit and take the uphill road out of the village to a gate and stile. Continue by a stony track through woods. Where the track levels, fork right onto a good path. Cross a stile on the right skyline and ascend the ridge, grass then rock, to a **grass plateau**. Scramble easily up the right side of the ridge to the summit of **Cnicht**.

Descend the north-east ridge, crossing or by-passing subsidiary summits, to a cairn at the far side of a **shallow col**. Turn right and follow a path (some vague sections) to **ruined quarry buildings** on the saddle between **Cwm Croesor** and **Cwm Orthin** (Variant (a) turns right here). Ascend an incline to enter the upper, boggy plateau. Continue along the path (occasional marker stones) then trend right to ascend the shallow north ridge of **Moelwyn Mawr**, identified by a series of small quartz outcrops. Trend rightwards near the top to gain the summit (Variant (b) descends west from here).

Go about 100m east from the summit then turn right and descend the south ridge, across the rocky subsidiary summit of **Craig Ysgafn**, to the pronounced col of **Bwlch Stwlan** (Variant (c) descends west from here).

Avoid crags of **Moelwyn Bach** by ascending a scree path diagonally up to the left to arrive on its grassy east spur. Turn right and ascend to the summit.

Descend the grassy west ridge and continue by a good path over lower pastures to a surfaced road. Turn right and walk along the road back to **Croesor** in a little over 1.5km.

Variant (a):

Turn right at quarry buildings on the saddle and descend a diagonal path across the southern side of **Cwm Croesor** to a road in the valley bottom. Turn right at crossroads to return to the start.

Variant (b):

Descend the ridge westwards from summit of **Moelwyn Mawr** to a final vague section leading down to a surfaced road. Turn right and return to start in less than 0.5km.

Variant (c):

Turn right at **Bwlch Stwlan** and follow a path below the north flank of **Moelwyn Bach's** west ridge. Rejoin the normal descent route at the base of the ridge.

14: EIFIONYDD

On a clear day the mountain panorama viewed from the summit of Snowdon will set your eyes flickering like undamped compass needles. There is so much to see. Eventually they will settle pointing in a north-easterly direction, irresistably drawn by the Glyders or Moel Siabod. A cluster of hills to the south-west, hazily backlit by the after-noon sun, will probably be dismissed are mere foothills. In fact these 'foothills' are a source of great delight to all who take the trouble to climb them.

Moel Hebog, prominent above Beddgelert, receives most walking traffic. Many are content to go straight up and down, but there is an excellent ridge extension (14.1) for those confident in their ability to negotiate the descent through a maze of forest trails.

The Nantlle Ridge is well known among ridge-walking enthusiasts. Downward views from its trembling crest reveal vegetated precipices shunned by sheep and rock climbers alike. A double traverse (14.3) prolongs interest and solves the logistical problems of arranging return transport.

Access is a sensitive issue in this area so it is as well to avoid improvising routes away from the described paths.

14.1 MOEL HEBOG AND MOEL LEFN FROM BEDDGELERT

Summary:
A strenuous ascent to an isolated peak followed by pleasant ridge-walking and a claustrophobic return through forests. Contrasting views of hills and coast. A 1:25,000 scale map is extremely useful for route-finding in the forest. Note than an ascent of Moel Hebog is rewarding by itself (return by the same route).

Duration:
12km and 950m height gain – allow 5–6hrs (includes descent time).

Terrain:
Grass, boulders, forest tracks and trails. Several boggy sections.

Approach:
From **Beddgelert**. Take the Porthmadog road (**A498**) from the junction in the village centre and turn right after just

EIFIONYDD

100m
to a car
park (fee)
at GR: 588
482.

Ascent & Descent:

Exit onto playing fields from
the north end of the car park. Turn right immediately and
cross the river by a footbridge to the main road (**A4085** to
Caernarfon). Turn left and walk up the road for about
400m. Turn left and follow a track for a little under 1km
(ignoring a right turn in trees) to buildings at **Cwm Cloch**.

Cross a ladder stile on the right and follow the path,
initially over wet ground then rising through ferns, to gain
the north-east ridge. Follow a stony path up the broad
ridge crest, trending left as crags come into view, to con-
front a steep boulder flank.

Follow a winding path up through boulders – some
easy scrambling – finishing over unpleasant scree. Emerge
at two prominent **cairns** (important indicators during the
descent of this route). Turn left and ascend the ridge with
some simple scrambling to the summit trig point of **Moel
Hebog**.

129

Marsh pools

Descend north-west down steep grass, keeping to the right of a stone wall, to a **deep col**. Ascend through the cleft in the outcrop above to pools. Avoid a crag on its right side and scramble over boulders to the summit of **Moel yr Ogof**.

Descend north-west, stepping over a fence at its junction with a stone wall, to grass. Continue along the ridge, soon rising to the rock spine of **Moel Lefn**.

Continue northwards, descending a steep path right (on grass) then left (boulders) to avoid cliffs. The ridge is now less distinct. Trend slightly right to a quarried hole. Descend steeply on the left side of a stone wall to the **col**. Turn right through a break in the wall and cross a fence by a stile to **enter the forest**.

Now the trouble starts (feel free to improvise if you think you can do better). Descend a muddy break to a track. Turn left and follow the track for a little under 100m. Turn right at a cairn to follow a narrow path over a footbridge and through trees. Emerge at a stile with **open ground** ahead.

Cross **open ground** by a narrow path – boggy and vague in places – to **re-enter the forest** at a stile. Continue through trees to a track. Turn left and follow the track, which bends right then left. Leave it at the second bend and descend through trees. Emerge at yet another track. Go 5m right then turn left to follow a narrow path. Cross directly over the next two tracks encountered to a **wide stream**.

Do not ford the stream but turn left and descend a rough track to a maintained forestry track. Turn right and follow it across the stream. Let's hope you are now entering a **forest camp site**. If so, turn left immediately and follow a track to the main road. Turn right here and walk back to **Beddgelert** in about 1.5km.

14.2 TRUM Y DDYSGL FROM RHYD DDU

Summary:
A tiring ascent up steep grass rewarded by excellent ridge-walking and simple scrambling. Ideal for a short day.

Duration:
9km and 600m height gain – allow 3–4hrs (includes descent time).

Terrain:
Mainly grass path (some boggy sections) with short sections of rock scrambling. Forest trails and tracks to finish.

Approach:
From Caernarfon or Beddgelert along the **A4085** to a large car park on the main road, 0.5km south of **Rhyd Ddu** village (GR: 571 526).

Ascent & Descent:
Go through a swing gate opposite the car park entrance and follow the slate path to a stream. Ignore the bridge directly ahead and turn left to cross a second footbridge and ladder stile. White markers guide you onto a track and so to a junction with the Nantlle road.

Turn left immediately, through a swing gate (footpath sign), and follow a path to the grassy flank of **Y Garn**. Turn right soon after crossing a ladder stile ('ridge' marked on a rock) and ascend steeply by a narrow path to the summit of **Y Garn**.

Follow the ridge southwards. It soon becomes narrow and rocky, but stay near the crest for maximum scrambling interest (though not on windy days!) to the undistinguished summit of **Mynydd Drws y Coed**.

Continue along the narrow ridge as it descends then veers rights and ascends to the equally unremarkable summit of **Trum y Ddysgl**.

Follow the grass ridge south-west, but soon fork left (14.3 forks right here) to descend the crest of an initially steep grass ridge (narrow path) to the boggy col of **Bwlch y Ddwy Elor**.

Go over a stile on the left and follow a good path and track, entering trees, to emerge later at a forestry track. Follow it rightwards for a few metres then bear left on a track leading to a stream. Cross the stream by a bridge on the left and then turn right onto the main track. After a few metres turn left and follow a rough stony path northwards across the base of the eastern slopes of **Mynydd Drws y Coed** and **Y Garn**. Enter a boggy area beyond a swing gate, but then continue on a good path to rejoin the ascent route at the painted rock.

14.3 NANTLLE RIDGE

Summary:
Delightful ridge-walking on grass, enlivened at intervals by sections of simple rock scrambling. Described as a

double traverse, returning to the start point (single traverse described as a variant).

Duration:
18km and 1300m height gain – allow 7–8hrs (includes descent time).

Terrain:
Mainly good paths over grass. Some rock scrambling.

Approach:
As for 14.2.

Ascent & Descent:
As for 14.2 to the summit of **Trum y Ddysgl**.
    Follow the grass ridge south-west then fork right (14.2 forks left here), descending, to cross a narrow neck leading up to the obelisk at the summit of **Mynydd**

Tal y Mignedd.
    Follow a broad grass ridge southwards and descend steeply on a collapsing path to the elongated col of **Bwlch Dros Bern**. Ascend the ridge ahead, scrambling up rocks just right of the crest (easiest line not obvious). A good path beyond winds up to the summit area of **Craig Cwm Silyn**.

133

Follow a broad and featureless ridge south-west to the final summit of **Garnedd Goch** (Variant (a) descends from here). If it is misty you could save time and avoid getting lost by ignoring the traverse to this final summit.

Return to **Rhyd Ddu** by the same route.

Variant (a):
For the single traverse it helps to leave a second vehicle at the road end at GR: 496 511 (park near the track in a field just beyond the gate). Follow the main route to **Garnedd Goch**. Descend a grass shoulder northwards to a **gate** in

*Nantlle Ridge
(route 14.3)*

the transverse stone wall. Go through the **gate** and turn left to follow the track to the road end, where your return transport will be parked (you hope).

14.4 MYNYDD MAWR FROM SNOWDON RANGER

Summary:
Pleasant walking over an isolated mountain. Ideal for a short day. Return by the ascent route if mist descends, or if trackless terrain on the described descent does not appeal.

Duration:
11km and 550m height gain – allow 4hrs (includes descent time).

Terrain:
Forest trails, grass and heather. Some boggy sections. 3.5km of road walking.

Approach:

Y Garn (left), taken by route 14.2, and Mynydd Mawr (route 14.4) from Rhyd Ddu

From Caernarfon or Beddgelert along the **A4085** to a large car park opposite the **Snowdon Ranger Youth Hostel** (GR: 565 551).

Ascent & Descent:
Turn right from the car park entrance and walk along the main road towards **Rhyd Ddu**. Turn right onto a forestry track at **farm** buildings, just after bridging the lake inflow.

Go through twin gates on the track then turn left immediately, through a gate, and ascend the pasture diagonally rightwards to enter the forest by a gate. Initially follow a good path through trees, then a poorer path along a break line to **emerge from the forest** at a ladder stile.

Turn right and ascend near the forest edge. The ascent ridge is better defined where the **forest ends**. Go up the ridge, quite steep, to a large squat cairn on the promontory of **Foel Rudd**.

Turn left and follow the undulating ridge crest (impressive views left down to **Craig y Bera**), finally curving rightwards to reach the circle shelter at the summit of **Mynydd Mawr**.

Descend north-west, first over stones then over heather slopes, to discover the clifftop path above **Cwm Du**. Turn left to descend this path, curving north, to a **mine** entrance.

Turn right and descend north-east then east, initially down a scree tongue then across pathless tufted heather, cursing, to the stream which drains **Cwm Du**. Turn left and follow the left bank of the stream to where it dives under a stone wall. Turn left by the wall and follow it to a small gate on the right, just beyond sheep folds.

Go over the ladder stile adjacent to the gate and cross the field between folds and trees/fence, over the stream, to a stile in the far corner. Cross the stile and continue by a pleasant path which soon descends through trees to a gate at the forest edge.

Go through the gate and descend to a track. Turn left and follow it to the main road. Turn right and follow the road back to the start in just over 2km.

15: SOUTHERN
SNOWDONIA

Comparatively few hill walkers travel to the large upland region of southern Snowdonia, and yet there is much to explore between scattered major peaks. The small selection of routes described here, while merely hinting at the potential, serves to introduce the area.

The 25km Rhinog Ridge extends from Llyn Trawsfynydd in the north to Barmouth in the south. It is renowned for its ankle-twisting boulder traps concealed by heather. In fact the truly awkward terrain is confined to the north; the southern section consists mostly of sheep-grazed turf. 15.1 sneaks up to a col in the middle of the ridge and ascends a heathery, but not too bouldery, Rhinog Fawr – the most prominent peak of the ridge.

Cader Idris was hewn from more conventional stuff. Rock ridges radiate outwards from the summit, circling above cliffs and enclosing lake-filled cwms. A popular path ascends gradually from the north (15.2), whereas a more entertaining route struggles up wooded slopes in the south to follow a scenic ridge (15.3).

Acute access problems interfere with hill walking in the Arans. A ridge path has been negotiated from Llanuwchllyn in the north to Cwm Cywarch in the south (15.4), but many walkers have been deterred by transport complications. More recently the negotiators have secured a circular route from Cwm Cywarch (Variant (a)). This incorporates Aran Fawddwy, the highest summit of the ridge.

The road east from Ffestiniog crosses moorland more typical of North Yorkshire than North Wales. Arenig Fawr rises from the east side of the moor with uncharacteristic steepness. 15.5 ascends the most interesting flank of the mountain to a summit from which, on a good day, every major hill group in Snowdonia can be seen.

15.1 RHINOG FAWR VIA
THE ROMAN STEPS

Summary:
A pleasant stroll through woodland and along an unusual rock pavement, culminating in a brief struggle with stones

and heather. Not recommended in misty weather because of problems with detailed route-finding.

Duration:
7km and 575m height
gain – allow 3–4hrs
(includes descent time).

Terrain:
Good path and rock pavement.
Scrambling (easy but scruffy).
Narrow path through heather and
boulders.

Approach:
From Harlech or Barmouth along the A496 to Llanbedr. Turn inland to follow a minor road on the north side of the river into **Cwm Bychan**. Park at the roadhead in **Cwm Bychan** (GR: 645 314).

Ascent & Descent:
Turn right from the roadhead on a track signposted to the **Roman Steps**. Continue through woods and follow the rock pavement of the Steps to the col of **Bwlch Tyddiad**.

Turn right from a little way beyond the highest point of the col and ascend a rough path up to the right. Continue over heathery slopes, ascending more or less directly, passing a small pool before gaining a minor summit.

Pass to the right (west) of **Llyn Du** to reach a stone wall. Continue by the side of the wall, ascending southwards, until the path bears left. Follow it, zig-zagging up to the summit and near-by trig point.

Return by the same route.

Resting at Bwlch Tyddiad before the arduous ascent of Rhinog Fawr (route 15.1)

Variant (a):
Descend a blunt ridge east, south-east, then south, to the heather-filled col of **Bwlch Drws Ardudwy**. Turn right and descend the path south-west (some boggy sections) to the roadhead in **Cwm Nantcol**.

15.2 CADER IDRIS FROM THE NORTH

Summary:
A pleasant woodland approach followed by a featureless track over the broad back of the mountain.

Duration:
4.5km and 750m height gain – allow 3hrs plus descent time (2hrs by this route).

Terrain:
Good paths over grass (one boggy section) then stones.
Short rocky section near the top.

Approach:
From Dolgellau on the A470. Leave the by-pass and enter
Dolgellau itself. Leave the town initially by the A493
(west) but turn left after a few hundred metres and follow
a minor road, passing the **Gwernan Lake hotel**. Finally
turn right on a track, about 1km beyond the hotel, to a
large car park at GR: 697 153.

Ascent:
Return to the surfaced road and turn right. Walk along the
road for about 100m then turn left (just before the second
bridge) onto a track. Go along the track then trend right on
a marked woodland path through gates and over
footbridges.

Continue pleasantly over more open country (some gaps
in the path but the line is obvious), finally ascending
steeply by a constructed zig-zag path towards the col. Go
though a gap in an old wall and over a ladder stile to the
col proper.

*View over the crags of
Cyfrwy from near the
summit of Pen y Gadair
(route 15.2)*

Turn left and follow a well-marked path (initially boggy) up the south flank of the broad ridge. The path eventually converges on the rim of the northern cwm. Circle the rim and ascend over rocks to the summit (there is a roofed **shelter** about 30m to the north).

Descent:
There are no route-finding complications (refer to the ascent notes).

Alternative Descents:
(1) Descent 15.3, having made arrangements for return transport. (2) Combination with the Fox's Path would make a convenient circular route. Unfortunately it descends a severely eroded and unstable scree slope in the upper region. The route is best avoided altogether.

15.3 CADER IDRIS FROM MINFFORDD

Summary:
A strenuous ascent through trees followed by an interesting ridge walk which circles a hidden cwm. Avoid a descent by Variant (a) in misty weather because of route-finding difficulties.

Duration:
4.5km and 900m height gain – allow 3hrs plus descent time (2–3hrs by this route).

Terrain:
Mainly good paths over grass, stones and rock. Some boggy sections.

Approach:
From Dolgellau or Machynlleth along the **A487**. Large car park at **Minffordd** (GR: 733 115), near the junction of the **B4405** to Abergynolwyn.

Ascent:
Walk down the Abergynolwyn road for a few hundred metres. Enter by the Idris Gates and follow a track over a footbridge. Zig-zag steeply up through trees on the left bank of the stream

to open ground where the angle eases. Continue along the path as it circles left and enters **Cwm Cau**.

Trend left from a large cairn, up a stony path, to gain the ridge crest on the left. Continue by the ridge crest, circling rightwards around the head of the cwm to the summit of **Mynydd Pencoed**.

Continue circling the cwm, initially descending to a low col then rising steeply to the summit of **Pen y Gadair**.

Descent:
There are no route-finding complications in good weather (refer to the ascent notes).

Alternative Descents:
(1) Descend 15.2, having made arrangements for return transport. (2) A descent by Variant (a) provides the most convenient alternative.

Variant (a):
Descend north-east over boulders from the summit of **Pen y Gadair**. Walk along the north edge of the broad ridge (avoid straying onto northern spurs) to the summit of **Mynydd Moel**.

Cross a stile to the east of the summit and then descend its broad southern spur, staying near the fence which follows its crest. The path asserts itself in the lower section and trends right to regain the approach path immediately above the pine plantation.

15.4 ARAN RIDGE

Summary:
A classic ridge traverse. Interest soon develops after an unremarkable beginning. Arranging return transport is a problem. Variant (a) describes a circular route from Cwm Cywarch. Access is a sensitive issue in the Arans; at present there is no scope for improvising alternative routes.

Duration:
15km and 800m height gain – allow 5–6hrs (includes descent time).

Terrain:
Narrow paths over grass (one boggy section). A few rocky sections.

Approach:
From Bala or Dolgellau along the **A494**. Turn off on the

B4403 to **Llanuwchllyn**. Park at a lay-by on a sharp left bend, about 1km after leaving the **A494** (GR: 880 297).

Ascent & Descent:
Cross a stile at the lay-by and follow the waymarked route onto the ridge (initially by a track then rightwards over pastures). Ascend the ridge, mostly on its west flank, by a narrow path over grass then stones to the summit of **Aran Benllyn**.

Continue along the ridge crest to the trig point and bouldery summit of **Aran Fawddwy**.

Proceed south-west along the ridge to a cairned promontory. Continue in the same line to a fence junction. Cross the left-hand of two stiles and turn left onto a rough path near the fence. Follow the path down **Drws Bach** onto a prominent grass ridge extending eastwards. Follow the fence along the ridge, later veering right and descending to a level area. Turn right and descend an obvious path which slants diagonally down the south-east flank of **Hengwm**.

Continue along the path, now sunken beneath a hawthorn arch (at one point there is a sharp detour right). Finally cross a footbridge onto the **Cwm Cywarch** road. Turn left to gain the parking place described in Variant (a).

Variant (a):
Approach via **Dinas Mawddwy** on the **A470**. Take the minor road through the village and continue north-east. Turn left after about 1km and follow the single track road signposted to **Cwm Cywarch**. After crossing a cattle grid, the road enters a meadow; park carefully at its far side, where a

(map continued on next page)

(continued from previous page)

track bears off to the left (GR: 854 185).

Continue to the roadhead. Detour rightwards around a **farm** (way-marked) and then trend rightwards to cross a ladder stile. Turn left immediately and follow a path which ascends the hillside left of a stream. Later cross the stream by a

15.4

foot-bridge and ascend its rocky right bank to a **boggy col**. Turn right and follow the path to the right of a fence (markers), passing a group of stiles, to a second set of stiles. Go over the stile and continue uphill to **Aran Fawddwy** summit. Return to **Cwm Cywarch** via the main route.

15.5 ARENIG FAWR

Summary:
A circular walk over an isolated mountain. Panoramic views of all major mountain groups in Snowdonia. Return by the ascent route if the marsh and road walk of the circular route do not appeal.

Duration:
12km and 550m height gain – allow 4–5hrs (includes descent time).

Terrain:
Stony track then narrow paths over grass and rock. Pathless grass and marsh on the descent. Track and road to finish.

Approach:
From Bala or Trawsfynydd along the **A4212**. Turn south on a minor road, almost opposite the **B4391** junction to Ffestiniog. Follow it eastwards for about 3km to a parking

View south from the summit of Arenig Fawr (route 15.5). The Aran ridge can be seen in the distance on the left

space (four cars) at GR: 846 396, opposite the track leading up to **Llyn Arenig Fawr**.

Ascent & Descent:
Follow the stony track (gate and stile at the start) to the **dam** at **Llyn Arenig Fawr**.

Cross the **dam** wall, ford the outflow, and ascend a narrow path onto the ridge beyond the lake. Ascend the ridge, grass then heather and rocks, to a level area with boulders. Step over a fence (blocks in place) and continue along the path to a **boggy plateau**.

Follow a narrow path, boggy in places, leading left-wards across the south-east flank of the summit ridge. Where the path (now barely more than a sheep track) begins to lose height, turn right and ascend steeply up to the ridge. Turn left and follow the stony crest up to the trig point, circle shelter and memorial stone at the summit.

Retrace the route of ascent, back down the ridge, but now continue north-east along it to a minor top and junction of fences. Step over the fence (blocks), turn left, and descend the ridge leading north-west. Stay on the right side of the electric fence (or intervening stone wall) throughout – down a steep section and across a **marsh** – to gain transverse **track**.

Turn right and follow the **track** to a gate near **sheepfolds** and large trees. Go down onto the dismantled **railway** and follow it rightwards, dodging ghost trains as necessary. When almost opposite the roadbridge, quit the **railway** for the track on the right. Follow this to a junction with the minor approach road. Turn right and regain the start after about 2km of road walking.

APPENDIX:
WELSH PLACE NAMES

In general:
- voice the vowel sounds in a *pure* rather than shaped fashion
- stress the penultimate syllable
- assume spelling is phonetic.

Vowel sounds:

short:

a	as in rat
e	as in pen
i	as in pin
o	as in top
u	as in swim
w	as in foot
y	as in rim
y	as in nurse (the words *y* and *yr* also use this sound)

long:

a	as in barb
e	as in dale
i	as in seen
o	as in shore
u	as in bean
w	as in tool
y	as in mean

Consonants:

b	
c	as in cap
ch	as in the German nacht
d	
dd	as in the

f	as in o*f*
ff	as in o*ff*
g	as in *g*o
ng	as in si*ng*
h, l	
ll	as hissed *l* sound
m, n, p, ph	
r	as in English, but trilled
rh	as in English, but with a stronger emission of breath
s	as in *s*it
si	as in *sh*op
t	
th	as in *th*ought

GLOSSARY OF COMMONLY USED PLACE NAMES

aber	river mouth
afon	river
aran	high place
bach	small, little
bont	bridge
bryn	hill
bwlch	col
cae	field
capel	chapel
carn/carnedd	cairn/heap
castell	castle
cau	hollow
clogwyn	cliff
coch	red
coed	trees, wood
craig	crag
crib	comb (sharp ridge)
cribin	rake (rocky ridge)
cwm	hollow, valley, cirque
dau, dwy	two
drws	door
du, ddu	black
dwr	water
dyffryn	valley

esgair	ridge
fach	small, little
fawr	large, big, great
ffordd	road
ffynnon	spring, well
foel	rounded/bare hill
garn/garnedd	cairn/heap
glas	blue (green)
goch	red
glyn	valley
gwyn, gwen	white
gwynt	wind
hafod	summer dwelling
hendre	winter dwelling
isaf	lower, lowest
llan	church, village
llwybr	path
llyn	lake
maen	stone, block
maes	field, meadow
main	narrow
mawr	large, big, great
moch	pigs
moel	rounded/bare hill
mynydd	mountain
nant	brook
newydd	new
ogof	cave
pen	head, top
pont	bridge
pwll	pool
rhaedr	waterfall
rhiw	hill, slope
rhos	moor
rhyd	ford
tal	front, end
tri	three
trum	ridge, summit
twll	hole
ty	house
tyddyn	small farm, cottage

uchaf	upper, highest
un	one
wen	white
y, yr	the
yn	in

LISTING OF CICERONE GUIDES

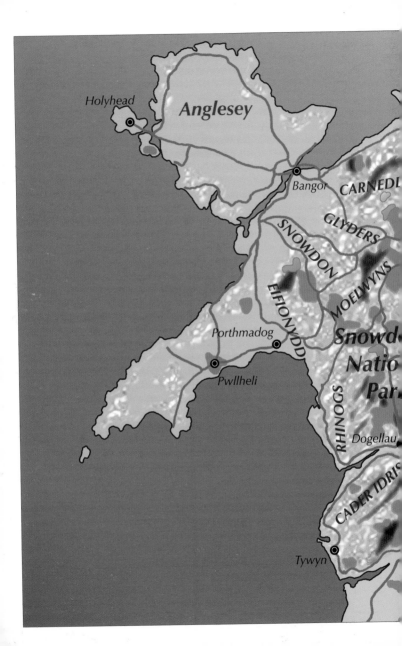